BASEBALL
TOP 10

STANDARD BERRA

Yankees catcher Yogi Berra appeared in more World Series games than any other player. Here he applies the tag in a play from the 1950 World Series.

MAJOR LEAGUE BASEBALL

BASEBALL TOP 10

Written and compiled by
James Buckley, Jr. and David Fischer

DK Publishing, Inc.

CONTENTS

LONDON, NEW YORK, MUNICH, MELBOURNE, and DELHI

Project Editor Beth Sutinis
Art Editor Megan Clayton
Creative Director Tina Vaughan
Publisher Andrew Berkhut
Production Chris Avgherinos

Produced by
Shoreline Publishing Group LLC
Santa Barbara, California
Editorial Director James Buckley, Jr.
Designer Tom Carling, Carling Design, Inc.

Produced in partnership and licensed by
Major League Baseball Properties, Inc.
Executive Vice President Timothy J. Brosnan
Vice President of Publishing Don Hintze
Major League Baseball Properties, Inc.
245 Park Avenue, New York, New York 10167

Second American Edition, 2004
04 05 06 07 08 10 9 8 7 6 5 4 3 2 1

Published in the United States by DK Publishing, Inc., 375 Hudson Street,
New York, New York 10014

Copyright © 2002 DK Publishing, Inc.
Text copyright © 2002 James Buckley, Jr.

DK Publishing, Inc. offers special discounts for bulk purchases for
sales promotions or premiums. Specific, large-quantity
needs can be met with special editions, including
personalized covers, excerpts of existing guides, and
corporate imprints. For more information, contact Special
Markets Department, DK Publishing, Inc., 375 Hudson
Street, New York, New York 10014

Library of Congress Cataloging-in-Publication Data

Baseball top 10

p. cm.

Summary: A compendium of more than two hundred twenty-five top
ten lists about baseball, covering such topics as most career strikeouts and
highest percentage of Hall of Fame votes received.

ISBN 0-7894-8506-0 (pbk.)

1. Baseball—Records—United States—Juvenile literature. 2. Baseball—
United States—History—Juvenile literature. [1. Baseball—Records.] I. Title:
Baseball top 10. II. Title: Baseball top ten.

GV877.4.M53 2002

796.357—dc21

2001047621

Reproduced by Colourscan, Singapore.
Printed and bound in China by Toppan Printing Co., Ltd

Discover more at
www.dk.com

INTRODUCTION

Who's Number Ten?

You can probably name the player who has hit the most career home runs (if you can't, turn to page 10), or the pitcher with the most career victories (page 17). But can you name the player with the fifth-most homers? Or the 10th? Or the pitcher with the seventh-most wins? Well, this book is here to make sure that you can come up with those answers and hundreds more like them. By providing more than 225 top 10 lists of stats and trivia, *Baseball Top 10* proves that there is more to life—and baseball statistics—than coming in first.

If you're like most baseball fans, you're simply crazy for statistics. You absorb stats like a sponge sucks up water, and you spout them like a broken fountain. If that's you, then welcome to paradise. *Baseball Top 10* covers every part of the game—past and present, on and off the field, from the Majors to Little League. No matter what your favorite part of baseball is (or what your favorite team is), you'll find something in here that's right up your alley.

Where did we find this stuff?

We looked high and low (and everywhere in between) to find the names and numbers in this book. Our main source was Major League Baseball itself, of course, through their comprehensive Web site, *www.mlb.com*. The Elias Sports Bureau provides all the official stats for MLB, and this book reflects Elias's calculations and listings on the site. Another key source was the seventh edition of *Total Baseball* (Total/Sports Illustrated, 2001), the official encyclopedia of MLB. At more than 2,500 pages, it was invaluable to our search for baseball beyond Number One. More information about the sources is available on page 96. Also, note that the information in this edition of *Baseball Top 10*, including career totals for players and teams and World Series information, is completely updated through the 2003 postseason.

So, dig in. Have fun. Stump your friends and neighbors. We think you'll find a lot more than ten ways to enjoy *Baseball Top 10*.

PLAYERS

GOLDEN ARM

Rocket-armed catcher Ivan Rodriguez is one of several current players who have won multiple Gold Glove awards for fielding excellence.

MAJOR AWARDS

Most Cy Young Awards

PITCHER (SEASONS)	AWARDS
1 **Roger Clemens** (1986, '87, '91, '97, '98, 2001)	6
2 **Randy Johnson** (1995, '99, 2000, '01, '02)	5
3= **Steve Carlton** (1972, '77, '80, '82)	4
= **Greg Maddux** (1992, '93, '94, '95)	4
5= **Pedro Martinez** (1997, '99, 2000)	3
= **Sandy Koufax** (1963, '65, '66)	3
= **Tom Seaver** (1969, '73, '75)	3
= **Jim Palmer** (1973, '75, '76)	3
9= Five players tied with	2

The Cy Young Award was given to one pitcher a year 1956–67, and to one pitcher from each league since then.

Recent Triple Crown Batters

	PLAYER (SEASON)	HR	RBI	BA
1	**Carl Yastrzemski** (1967)	44	121	.326
2	**Frank Robinson** (1966)	49	122	.316
3	**Mickey Mantle** (1956)	52	130	.353
4	**Ted Williams** (1947)	32	114	.343
5	**Ted Williams** (1942)	36	137	.356
6	**Joe Medwick** (1937)	31	154	.374
7	**Lou Gehrig** (1934)	49	165	.363
8=	**Chuck Klein** (1933)	28	120	.368
=	**Jimmie Foxx** (1933)	48	163	.356
10	**Rogers Hornsby** (1925)	39	143	.403

The batting Triple Crown—leading a league in home runs, runs batted in, and batting average—is one of baseball's rarest hitting feats.

THE MICK
Slugging outfielder Mickey Mantle of the Yankees combined speed and power like few others in baseball history. He is the all-time leader in home runs by a switch-hitter.

Top 10 Most Recent A.L. Cy Young Awards
(Pitcher/Season)

❶ **Roy Halladay**, 2003 ❷ **Barry Zito**, 2002 ❸ **Roger Clemens**, 2001 ❹ **Pedro Martinez**, 2000 ❺ **Pedro Martinez**, 1999 ❻ **Roger Clemens**, 1998 ❼ **Roger Clemens**, 1997 ❽ **Pat Hentgen**, 1996 ❾ **Randy Johnson**, 1995 ❿ **David Cone**, 1994

Top 10 Most Recent N.L. Cy Young Awards
Pitcher/Season

❶ **Eric Gagne**, 2003 ❷ **Randy Johnson**, 2002 ❸ **Randy Johnson**, 2001 ❹ **Randy Johnson**, 2000 ❺ **Randy Johnson**, 1999 ❻ **Tom Glavine**, 1998 ❼ **Pedro Martinez**, 1997 ❽ **John Smoltz**, 1996 ❾ **Greg Maddux**, 1995 ❿ **Greg Maddux**, 1994

MARTINEZ MAGIC
In 1999, Pedro Martinez of the Red Sox became one of only three pitchers to win the Cy Young Award in each league. He is joined by Gaylord Perry and Randy Johnson in this elite club.

THE TOP 10

Recent A.L. Rookies of the Year

SEASON	PLAYER, TEAM
2003	**Angel Berroa**, Kansas City Royals
2002	**Eric Hinske**, Toronto Blue Jays
2001	**Ichiro Suzuki**, Seattle Mariners
2000	**Kazuhiro Sasaki**, Seattle Mariners
1999	**Carlos Beltran**, Kansas City Royals
1998	**Ben Grieve**, Oakland A's
1997	**Nomar Garciaparra**, Red Sox
1996	**Derek Jeter**, New York Yankees
1995	**Marty Cordova**, Minn. Twins
1994	**Bob Hamelin**, Kansas City Royals

The Rookie of Year is also voted on by the BBWAA. The winner receives the Jackie Robinson Award, named for the great Dodgers' player who in 1947 became the first African-American player in the Majors in the 20th century. Robinson was named the rookie of the year that season while playing first base, though he later moved to second base.

THE TOP 10

Recent N.L. Rookies of the Year

SEASON	PLAYER, TEAM
2003	**Dontrelle Willis**, Florida Marlins
2002	**Jason Jennings**, Colorado Rockies
2001	**Albert Pujols**, St. Louis Cardinals
2000	**Rafael Furcal**, Atlanta Braves
1999	**Scott Williamson**, Cin. Reds
1998	**Kerry Wood**, Chicago Cubs
1997	**Scott Rolen**, Philadelphia Phillies
1996	**Todd Hollandsworth**, Dodgers
1995	**Hideo Nomo**, Los Angeles Dodgers
1994	**Raul Mondesi**, Los Angeles Dodgers

THE TOP 10

Recent N.L. MVPs

SEASON	PLAYER, TEAM
2003	**Barry Bonds**, San Francisco Giants
2002	**Barry Bonds**, San Francisco Giants
2001	**Barry Bonds**, San Francisco Giants
2000	**Jeff Kent**, San Francisco Giants
1999	**Chipper Jones**, Atlanta Braves
1998	**Sammy Sosa**, Chicago Cubs
1997	**Larry Walker**, Colorado Rockies
1996	**Ken Caminiti**, San Diego Padres
1995	**Barry Larkin**, Cincinnati Reds
1994	**Jeff Bagwell**, Houston Astros

THE TOP 10

Recent A.L. MVPs

SEASON	PLAYER, TEAM
2003	**Alex Rodriguez**, Texas Rangers
2002	**Miguel Tejada**, Oakland A's
2001	**Ichiro Suzuki**, Seattle Mariners
2000	**Jason Giambi**, Oakland A's
1999	**Ivan Rodriguez**, Texas Rangers
1998	**Juan Gonzalez**, Texas Rangers
1997	**Ken Griffey, Jr.**, Seattle Mariners
1996	**Juan Gonzalez**, Texas Rangers
1995	**Mo Vaughn**, Boston Red Sox
1994	**Frank Thomas**, Chicago White Sox

QUIZ TIME
The single-season home run record is 73, set by Barry Bonds in 2001. But can you name the single-season record-holder for runs batted in? Answer on page 13.

9

HITTING STARS

Most Career Hits

BATTER (YEARS PLAYED)	HITS
1 **Pete Rose** (1963–86)	4,256
2 **Ty Cobb** (1905–28)	4,189
3 **Hank Aaron** (1954–76)	3,771
4 **Stan Musial** (1941–63)	3,630
5 **Tris Speaker** (1907–28)	3,514
6 **Honus Wagner** (1897–1917)	3,420
7 **Carl Yastrzemski** (1961–83)	3,419
8 **Paul Molitor** (1978–98)	3,319
9 **Eddie Collins** (1906–30)	3,315
10 **Willie Mays** (1951–73)	3,283

Three thousand hits is the standard for hitting greatness combined with longevity. These ten players are the top of a list of only 25 who have reached that total in baseball history. The great Roberto Clemente made it onto that exclusive list with a double in the last at-bat of his great career, before he was tragically killed in an airplane crash in 1972. An interesting note: Cobb for many years was credited with 4,191 hits, but recent scholarly research has resulted in the new career total for him listed above.

Most Career Total Bases

BATTER (YEARS PLAYED)	TOTAL BASES
1 **Hank Aaron** (1954–76)	6,856
2 **Stan Musial** (1941–63)	6,134
3 **Willie Mays** (1951–73)	6,066
4 **Ty Cobb** (1905–28)	5,854
5 **Babe Ruth** (1914–35)	5,793
6 **Pete Rose** (1963–86)	5,752
7 **Carl Yastrzemski** (1961–83)	5,539
8 **Eddie Murray** (1977–97)	5,397
9 **Frank Robinson** (1956–76)	5,373
10 **Barry Bonds*** (1986–)	5,253

Total bases are calculated quite simply: by adding up the number of bases a player reaches via base hits. A single is one base, a double two, and so on.

Most Career Home Runs

BATTER (YEARS PLAYED)	HOME RUNS
1 **Hank Aaron** (1954–76)	755
2 **Babe Ruth** (1914–35)	714
3 **Willie Mays** (1951–73)	660
4 **Barry Bonds*** (1986–)	658
5 **Frank Robinson** (1956–76)	586
6 **Mark McGwire** (1986–2001)	583
7 **Harmon Killebrew** (1954–75)	573
8 **Reggie Jackson** (1967–87)	563
9 **Mike Schmidt** (1972–89)	548
10 **Sammy Sosa*** (1989–)	539

HAMMERIN' HANK
On April 8, 1974, Hank Aaron became baseball's all-time home-run king when he slugged his 715th career home run off Dodgers pitcher Al Downing.

THE TOP 10
Highest Career Batting Average

BATTER (YEARS PLAYED)	BATTING AVERAGE
1 **Ty Cobb** (1905–28)	.366
2 **Rogers Hornsby** (1915–37)	.358
3 **Joe Jackson** (1908–20)	.356
4 **Dan Brouthers** (1879–1904)	.349
5 **Pete Browning** (1882–94)	.349
6 **Ed Delahanty** (1888–1903)	.346
7 **Tris Speaker** (1907–28)	.345
8 **Billy Hamilton** (1888–1901)	.344
9 **Ted Williams** (1939–60)	.344
10 **Babe Ruth** (1914–35)	.342

For many years, Cobb's average was recorded as .367. But diligent research by amateur, and later, Major League experts revealed errors in the record books that dropped the mark by .001 (see top 10 list for career hits, too). But that does nothing to detract from Cobb's outstanding batting skill.

A note on batting average: You'll see several places where players with the same average are not listed as tied. That's because batting averages can be calculated beyond three digits as shown; the fourth digit can break the tie.

THE TOP 10
Most Career Runs Batted In

BATTER (YEARS PLAYED)	RUNS BATTED IN
1 **Hank Aaron** (1954–76)	2,297
2 **Babe Ruth** (1914–35)	2,213
3 **Lou Gehrig** (1923–39)	1,995
4 **Stan Musial** (1941–63)	1,951
5 **Ty Cobb** (1905–28)	1,938
6 **Jimmie Foxx** (1925–45)	1,922
7 **Eddie Murray** (1977–97)	1,917
8 **Willie Mays** (1951–73)	1,903
9 **Cap Anson** (1876–97)	1,880
10 **Mel Ott** (1926–47)	1,860

THE TOP 10
Longest Hitting Streak

BATTER (SEASON)	CONSECUTIVE GAMES
1 **Joe DiMaggio**, Yankees (1941)	56
2= **Willie Keeler**, Orioles (1897)	44
= **Pete Rose**, Reds (1978)	44
4 **Bill Dahlen**, Cubs (1894)	42
5 **George Sisler**, Browns (1922)	41
6 **Ty Cobb**, Tigers (1911)	40
7 **Paul Molitor**, Brewers (1987)	39
8 **Tommy Holmes**, Braves (1945)	37
9 **Billy Hamilton**, Phillies (1894)	36
10= **Fred Clarke**, Louisville (1895)	35
= **Ty Cobb**, Tigers (1917)	35

In the endless debate over what records are "unbreakable," DiMaggio's amazing streak often tops the list. Though he was certainly under enormous pressure during the 56 games that his streak comprised, one can only imagine the immense weight of media and fan interest that would pummel a player today who even approached that mark. Pete Rose tied the all-time National League mark in 1978 under a constant glare of publicity that, too, pales to today's media madness.

THE TOP 10
Most Runs Scored in a Career

BATTER (YEARS PLAYED)	RUNS SCORED
1 **Rickey Henderson*** (1979–)	2,295
2 **Ty Cobb** (1905–28)	2,246
3= **Hank Aaron** (1954–76)	2,174
= **Babe Ruth** (1914–35)	2,174
5 **Pete Rose** (1963–86)	2,165
6 **Willie Mays** (1951–73)	2,062
7 **Stan Musial** (1941–63)	1,949
8 **Barry Bonds*** (1986–)	1,941
9 **Lou Gehrig** (1923–39)	1,888
10 **Tris Speaker** (1907–28)	1,882

DYNAMIC DUO
Lou Gehrig and Babe Ruth combined to form baseball's most powerful slugging twosome. They dominated baseball in the 1920s and 1930s, helping the Yankees win four titles.

THE TOP 10
Highest Career Slugging Average

BATTER (YEARS PLAYED)	SLUGGING AVERAGE
1 **Babe Ruth** (1914–35)	.690
2 **Ted Williams** (1939–60)	.634
3 **Lou Gehrig** (1923–39)	.632
4 **Jimmie Foxx** (1925–45)	.609
5 **Hank Greenberg** (1930–47)	.605
6 **Barry Bonds*** (1986–)	.602
7 **Manny Ramirez*** (1993–)	.598
8 **Mark McGwire** (1986–2001)	.588
9 **Joe DiMaggio** (1936–51)	.579
10 **Rogers Hornsby** (1915–37)	.577

Slugging average is calculated by dividing total bases by times at bat. A player who bats 50 times and has 30 total bases has a slugging average of .600. The number measures a player's ability to make extra-base hits, which are any hits except singles.

* Active through 2003

QUIZ TIME
Rickey Henderson took over the all-time lead in runs scored in 2001. In which two other major offensive categories is Henderson also the career leader? Answer on page 15.

SINGLE-SEASON RECORDS

Highest Slugging Average in a Season

BATTER (SEASON)	SLUGGING AVERAGE
1 Barry Bonds* (2001)	.863
2 Babe Ruth (1920)	.847
3 Babe Ruth (1921)	.846
4 Babe Ruth (1927)	.772
5 Lou Gehrig (1927)	.765
6 Babe Ruth (1923)	.764
7 Rogers Hornsby (1925)	.756
8 Mark McGwire (1998)	.752
9 Jeff Bagwell (1994)	.750
10 Jimmie Foxx (1932)	.749

GOIN' YARD

Mark McGwire thrilled the sports world in 1998 with his pursuit of the single-season home-run record. He obliterated the old mark of 61 with a stunning total of 70! But his record lasted only three seasons before Barry Bonds hit 73 in 2001.

Top Ten Total Bases in a Season

Batter (Season)/Total Bases

1 Babe Ruth (1921) 457 **2 Rogers Hornsby** (1922) 450 **3 Lou Gehrig** (1927) 447 **4 Chuck Klein** (1930) 445 **5 Jimmie Foxx** (1932) 438 **6 Stan Musial** (1948) 429 **7 Sammy Sosa** (2001) 425 **8 Hack Wilson** (1930) 423 **9 Chuck Klein** (1932) 420 **10** = **Lou Gehrig** (1930) 419; = **Luis Gonzalez** (2001) 419

Most Runs Scored in a Season

BATTER (SEASON)	RUNS SCORED
1 Billy Hamilton (1894)	198
2 =Tom Brown (1891)	177
=Babe Ruth (1921)	177
4 =Tip O'Neill (1887)	167
=Lou Gehrig (1936)	167
6 Billy Hamilton (1895)	166
7 =Willie Keeler (1894)	165
=Joe Kelley (1894)	165
9 =Arlie Latham (1887)	163
=Babe Ruth (1928)	163
=Lou Gehrig (1931)	163

Highest Batting Average in a Season

BATTER (SEASON)	BATTING AVERAGE
1 Tip O'Neill (1887)	.485
2 Pete Browning (1887)	.457
3 Bob Caruthers (1887)	.456
4 Hugh Duffy (1894)	.440
5 Yank Robinson (1887)	.427
6 Nap Lajoie (1901)	.426
7 Willie Keeler (1897)	.424
8 Rogers Hornsby (1924)	.424
9 Cap Anson (1887)	.421
10 Dan Brouthers (1887)	.420

DID YOU KNOW?

We don't have a list for lowest batting averages, but any player hitting under .200 is said to be hitting "below the Mendoza line," named for light-hitting shortstop Mario Mendoza.

Most Hits in a Season

Batter (Season)/Hits

1 = **Pete Browning** (1887), 275; = **Tip O'Neill** (1887), 275 **3** **George Sisler** (1920), 257 **4** **Denny Lyons** (1887), 256 **5** = **Lefty O'Doul** (1929), 254; = **Bill Terry** (1930), 254 **7** **Al Simmons** (1925), 253 **8** **Oyster Burns** (1887), 251 **9** = **Rogers Hornsby** (1922), 250; = **Chuck Klein** (1930), 250

Most Runs Batted In in a Season

	BATTER (SEASON)	RUNS BATTED IN
1	**Hack Wilson** (1930)	191
2	**Lou Gehrig** (1931)	184
3	**Hank Greenberg** (1937)	183
4	**Lou Gehrig** (1927)	175
=	**Jimmie Foxx** (1938)	175
6	**Lou Gehrig** (1930)	174
7	**Babe Ruth** (1921)	171
8	= **Chuck Klein** (1930)	170
=	**Hank Greenberg** (1935)	170
10	**Jimmie Foxx** (1932)	169

Most Home Runs in a Season

	BATTER (SEASON)	HOME RUNS
1	**Barry Bonds*** (2001)	73
2	**Mark McGwire*** (1998)	70
3	**Sammy Sosa*** (1998)	66
4	**Mark McGwire*** (1999)	65
5	**Sammy Sosa*** (2001)	64
6	**Sammy Sosa*** (1999)	63
7	**Roger Maris** (1961)	61
8	**Babe Ruth** (1927)	60
9	**Babe Ruth** (1921)	59
10	= **Mark McGwire** (1997)	58
=	**Jimmie Foxx** (1932)	58
=	**Hank Greenberg** (1938)	58

Highest OPS in a Season

	BATTER (SEASON)	OPS
1	**Babe Ruth** (1920)	1.379
2	**Barry Bonds*** (2001)	1.378
3	**Babe Ruth** (1921)	1.359
4	**Babe Ruth** (1923)	1.309
5	**Ted Williams** (1941)	1.286
6	**Ted Williams** (1957)	1.259
7	**Babe Ruth** (1927)	1.258
8	**Babe Ruth** (1926)	1.253
9	**Babe Ruth** (1924)	1.252
10	**Rogers Hornsby** (1925)	1.245

OPS is a fairly new addition to the list of statistics, and many experts feel it is the best measure of a player's overall hitting ability. OPS stands for on-base percentage plus slugging average. That is, it measures the two things a player must do well to excel: hit for average (i.e., get on base) and hit for power. Not surprisingly, Ruth again dominates this list. Barry Bonds's total of 1378 in his record-breaking 2001 season included a .515 on-base percentage, the highest in the Majors since 1957.

THE M&M BOYS

Thirty-seven years before Mark McGwire and Sammy Sosa created home run hysteria, a pair of New York Yankees did the same thing. In 1961, Roger Maris (left) and Mickey Mantle battled back and forth all summer long, with the pressure rising with each home run. In early September, with 54 home runs, Mantle fell seriously ill with an infection and had to sit out the rest of the season. Maris, though nearly overwhelmed with the attention, kept slugging, and on the last day of the season, hit his 61st home run, breaking Babe Ruth's record. At the time, he was criticized for doing it in 161 games to Ruth's 151, but the passage of time has earned Maris respect.

SNAP SHOTS

* Active through 2003

STREAKS AND STEALS

Most Consecutive Games Played

PLAYER (YEARS OF STREAK)	GAMES
1 Cal Ripken, Jr. (1981–2001)	2,316
2 Lou Gehrig (1925–39)	2,130
3 Everett Scott (1916–25)	1,307
4 Steve Garvey (1974–83)	1,207
5 Billy Williams (1963–70)	1,117
6 Joe Sewell (1922–30)	1,103
7 Stan Musial (1951–57)	895
8 Eddie Yost (1949–55)	829
9 Gus Suhr (1932–38)	822
10 Nellie Fox (1952–59)	798

Ripken's pursuit of Gehrig's incredible streak was one of the biggest baseball stories of the 1990s. Both players not only racked up an amazing string of games while overcoming the dozens of daily injuries, aches, and pains that go along with playing baseball, but both excelled as players and as leaders off the field.

Career Games Played, All Time

PLAYER (YEARS PLAYED)	GAMES
1 Pete Rose (1963–86)	3,562
2 Carl Yastrzemski (1961–83)	3,308
3 Hank Aaron (1954–76)	3,298
4 Ty Cobb (1905–28)	3,035
5 =Eddie Murray (1977–97)	3,026
=Stan Musial (1941–63)	3,026
7 Cal Ripken, Jr.* (1981–2001)	3,001
8 Willie Mays (1951–73)	2,992
9 Rickey Henderson* (1979–)	2,979
10 Dave Winfield (1973–95)	2,973

Most Consecutive Seasons Played with One Team

PLAYER, TEAM	SEASONS
1 =Brooks Robinson, Orioles	23
=Carl Yastrzemski, Red Sox	23
3 =Cap Anson, Cubs	22
=Ty Cobb, Tigers	22
=Al Kaline, Tigers	22
=Stan Musial, Cardinals	22
=Mel Ott, Giants	22
=Hank Aaron, Braves	21
9 =George Brett, Royals	21
=Harmon Killebrew, Senators/Twins	21
=Willie Mays, Giants	21
=Willie Stargell, Pirates	21
=Cal Ripken, Jr.*, Orioles	21

With the advent of free agency and the increased player movement of recent decades, a player spending his entire career with one team has become more of a rarity, thus few players playing today have much real chance of cracking this list.

Career Games Played, Active

PLAYER	SEASONS
1 Cal Ripken, Jr.	3,001
2 Rickey Henderson	2,979
3 Harold Baines	2,830
4 Tony Gwynn	2,440
5 Tim Raines	2,404
5 Barry Bonds	2,296
6 Rafael Palmeiro	2,258
7 Fred McGriff	2,201
9 Tony Fernandez	2,158
10 Bobby Bonilla	2,113

This list reflects players who completed the 2001 season. Future Hall-of-Famers Ripken and Gwynn retired after the 2001 season.

DID YOU KNOW?
The most surprising play in baseball is often the steal of home plate. Rod Carew of the Twins stole home seven times in 1969, tying Pete Reiser's single-season record.

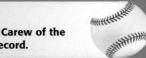

THE TOP 10

Most Career Stolen Bases

PLAYER (CAREER)	STOLEN BASES
1 Rickey Henderson* (1979–)	1,395
2 Lou Brock (1961–79)	938
3 Billy Hamilton (1888–1901)	914
4 Ty Cobb (1905–28)	892
5 Tim Raines* (1979–)	808
6 Vince Coleman (1985–97)	752
7 Eddie Collins (1906–30)	745
8 Arlie Latham (1880–1909)	742
9 Max Carey (1910–1929)	738
10 Honus Wagner (1897–1917)	723

IRON CAL
Cal Ripken, Jr., began his career as a third baseman, but later switched to shortstop, where he became a perennial All-Star. He later returned to third base, where he ended his career.

THE TOP 10

Highest Stolen Base Average in a Season

BASERUNNER (SEASON)	STOLEN BASE AVERAGE
1 =Kevin McReynolds (1988)	100.0
=Paul Molitor (1994)	100.0
3 =Brady Anderson* (1994)	96.9
=Carlos Beltran (2001)	96.9
5 Max Carey (1922)	96.2
6 Ken Griffey, Sr. (1980)	95.8
7 Stan Javier* (1988)	95.2
8 Doug Glanville* (1999)	94.4
9 Amos Otis (1970)	94.3
10 Jack Perconte (1985)	93.9

Note that making this list required stealing a minimum of 20 bases in a season. McReynolds was not known as a speedster, but he made the most of his attempts, being successful on 21 of 21 in 1988. Molitor stole 504 bases in his great career, including 20 for 20 in 1994. Pirates and Dodgers outfielder Max Carey is another all-time great in stolen bases, with 738 for his career.

THE TOP 10

Highest Career Stolen Base Average

PLAYER (YEARS PLAYED)	STOLEN BASE AVERAGE
1 Tony Womack* (1993–)	85.3
2 Tim Raines* (1979–)	84.6
3 Eric Davis* (1984–)	84.0
4 Henry Cotto (1984–93)	83.3
5 Barry Larkin* (1986–)	83.2
5 Willie Wilson (1976–94)	83.3
7 Davey Lopes (1972–87)	83.0
8 Stan Javier* (1984–)	82.8
9 Julio Cruz (1977–1986)	81.5
10 Joe Morgan (1963–1984)	81.0

This statistic is calculated by dividing the number of stolen bases by the number of stolen base attempts. Successful basestealers combine speed, timing, and careful study of pitchers' pickoff moves.

THE TOP 10

Most Stolen Bases in a Season

PLAYER (SEASON)	STOLEN BASES
1 Hugh Nicol (1887)	138
2 Rickey Henderson (1982)	130
3 Arlie Latham (1887)	129
4 Lou Brock (1974)	118
5 Charlie Comiskey (1887)	117
6 =John Ward (1887)	111
=Billy Hamilton (1889)	111
=Billy Hamilton (1891)	111
9 Vince Coleman (1985)	110
10 =Arlie Latham (1888)	109
=Vince Coleman (1987)	109

Rickey Henderson's 130 steals in 1982, the most in almost 100 years, is regarded as the modern Major League record.

THE IRON HORSE

Before Cal Ripken proved that unbreakable records can indeed be broken, Yankees first baseman Lou Gehrig was the standard by which all other "iron men" were judged. He stepped in for an ailing Wally Pipp in 1925 and didn't give up the job for 14 seasons. Among baseball's greatest all-time sluggers, Gehrig was almost universally liked by teammates and opponents. Thus when he was struck down by amyotrophic lateral sclerosis (ALS), a muscular and nervous system disease, the entire baseball world was saddened. The disease ended his career in 1939 and his life in 1941.

SNAP SHOTS

PITCHING ACES

Career Games Pitched

PITCHER (YEARS PLAYED)	GAMES
1 Jesse Orosco* (1979–)	1,131
2 Dennis Eckersley (1975–98)	1,071
3 Hoyt Wilhelm (1952–72)	1,070
4 Kent Tekulve (1974–89)	1,050
5 Lee Smith (1980–97)	1,022
6 Rich Gossage (1972–94)	1,002
7 John Franco* (1984–)	998
8 Lindy McDaniel (1955–75)	987
9 Dan Plesac* (1986–)	946
10 Rollie Fingers (1965–85)	944

UNBREAKABLE?

Cy Young averaged more than 23 wins per season during his 21-year career. Of course, he's also the all-time leader in losses with 316.

ROCKET MAN

Roger Clemens of the New York Yankees became the all-time leader for strikeouts in the American League during the 2001 season.

DID YOU KNOW?

In 1972, Philadelphia's Steve Carlton won 27 games (and the Cy Young Award). His Phillies won only 59 games. It was the highest-ever percentage of team wins by one pitcher.

THE TOP 10

Shutouts in a Career

PITCHER (YEARS PLAYED)	SHUTOUTS
1 Walter Johnson (1907–27)	110
2 Pete Alexander (1911–30)	90
3 Christy Mathewson (1900–16)	79
4 Cy Young (1890–1911)	76
5 Eddie Plank (1901–17)	69
6 Warren Spahn (1942–65)	63
7=Nolan Ryan (1966–93)	61
=Tom Seaver (1967–86)	61
9 Bert Blyleven (1970–92)	60
10 Don Sutton (1966–88)	58

A shutout is earned when a pitcher wins an official, complete game and the other team does not score a run.

THE TOP 10

Career Saves

PITCHER (YEARS PLAYED)	SAVES
1 Lee Smith (1980–97)	478
2 John Franco* (1984–)	422
3 Dennis Eckersley (1975–98)	390
4 Jeff Reardon (1979–94)	367
5 Randy Myers (1985–98)	347
6 Rollie Fingers (1968–85)	341
7 John Wetteland (1989–2000)	330
8 Rick Aguilera (1985–2000)	318
9 Trevor Hoffman* (1993–)	314
10 Tom Henke (1982–95)	311

A save is normally awarded to a pitcher who enters the game with the winning runs on deck, at the plate, or on the bases, and who then finishes the game without the other team tying the game or taking a lead. Notice that these top 10 leaders in saves all played after 1970, when the role of the relief pitcher began to be more prominent. By the early 1980s, each team usually had one "closer," who pitched only the ninth inning of games or a little more, resulting in increases in the number of saves awarded.

THE TOP 10

Career Wins

PITCHER (YEARS PLAYED)	WINS
1 Cy Young (1890–1911)	511
2 Walter Johnson (1907–27)	417
3=Pete Alexander (1911–30)	373
=Christy Mathewson (1900–16)	373
5 Warren Spahn (1942–65)	363
6=Jim Galvin (1875–92)	361
=Kid Nichols (1890–1906)	361
8 Tim Keefe (1880–93)	342
9 Steve Carlton (1965–88)	329
10 John Clarkson (1882–94)	328

THE TOP 10

Career Strikeouts by Pitcher

PITCHER (YEARS PLAYED)	STRIKEOUTS
1 Nolan Ryan (1966–93)	5,714
2 Steve Carlton (1965–88)	4,136
3 Roger Clemens* (1984–)	3,717
4 Bert Blyleven (1970–92)	3,701
5 Tom Seaver (1967–86)	3,640
6 Don Sutton (1966–88)	3,574
7 Gaylord Perry (1962–83)	3,534
8 Walter Johnson (1904–24)	3,508
9 Randy Johnson (1988–)	3,412
10 Phil Niekro (1964–87)	3,342

THE RYAN EXPRESS

Nolan Ryan threw longer than any pitcher in Major League history, and possibly harder. He began his career with an overpowering fastball, but he was never sure where it was going. He was as famous for his wildness as his 100-mph heater. As he matured as a pitcher, he combined power with precision. In 1973, he set the single-season record with 383 strikeouts. Ryan threw 7 no-hitters, more than any other pitcher.

THE TOP 10

Career Earned Run Average (ERA)

PITCHER (YEARS PLAYED)	ERA
1 Ed Walsh (1904–17)	1.82
2 Addie Joss (1902–10)	1.89
3 Mordecai Brown (1903–16)	2.06
4 John M. Ward (1878–84)	2.10
5 Christy Mathewson (1900–16)	2.13
6 Rube Waddell (1897–1910)	2.16
7 Walter Johnson (1907–27)	2.17
8 Orval Overall (1905–10, 1913)	2.23
9 Tommy Bond (1874–84)	2.25
10 Ed Reulbach (1905–17)	2.28

Earned run average is calculated by multiplying a pitcher's earned runs by 9, then dividing the result by the number of innings pitched. An earned run is charged to a pitcher as long as an error did not help the run score or the runner who scored to reach base.

Mordecai Brown was known as "Three Fingered." Brown earned his nickname the hard way, by losing a finger and parts of two others in a boyhood farming accident. He may have gained by the loss, however, as the movement on his fastball caused by his unusual hand may have helped him achieve success.

SNAP SHOTS

PITCHING ACES

Most Wins in a Season

	PITCHER (SEASON)	WINS
1	Charley Radbourn (1884)	59
2	John Clarkson (1885)	53
3	Guy Hecker (1884)	52
4	John Clarkson (1889)	49
5=	Charley Radbourn (1883)	48
=	Charlie Buffinton (1884)	48
7=	Al Spalding (1876)	47
=	John Ward (1879)	47
9=	Jim Galvin (1883)	46
=	Jim Galvin (1884)	46
=	Matt Kilroy (1887)	46

All these pitchers played before the "modern" era; the list below shows most victories in a season since 1900. Many of the pitchers above threw with the then-mandatory underhand motion.

Most Strikeouts in a Season

	PITCHER (SEASON)	STRIKEOUTS
1	Matt Kilroy (1886)	513
2	Toad Ramsey (1886)	499
3	Hugh Daily (1884)	483
4	Dupee Shaw (1884)	451
5	Charley Radbourn (1884)	441
6	Charlie Buffinton (1884)	417
7	Guy Hecker (1884)	385
8	Nolan Ryan (1973)	383
9	Sandy Koufax (1965)	382
10	Bill Sweeney (1884)	374

Again, comparisons of pre-1900s play with modern play are skewed by the huge difference in appearances by early pitchers. But note that Ryan and Koufax's totals were piled up in far fewer games, yet still approach all-time single-season bests. Ryan's 383 is the modern record.

Most Strikeouts per Nine Innings in a Season

	PITCHER (SEASON)	STRIKEOUTS
1	Randy Johnson (2001)	13.44
2	Pedro Martinez (1999)	13.20
3	Kerry Wood (1998)	12.58
4	Randy Johnson (2000)	12.56
5	Randy Johnson (1995)	12.35
6	Randy Johnson (1997)	12.30
7	Randy Johnson (1998)	12.12
8	Randy Johnson (1999)	12.06
9	Pedro Martinez (2000)	11.78
10	Nolan Ryan (1987)	11.48

Calculated by dividing a pitcher's innings by nine, to equal a full game, and then dividing that number into total strikeouts in a season, this is a great measure of a power pitcher's overpowering nature.

Most Wins in a Season Since 1900

	PITCHER (SEASON)	WINS
1	Jack Chesbro (1904)	41
2	Ed Walsh (1908)	40
3	Christy Mathewson (1908)	37
4	Joe McGinnity (1904)	35
5	Joe Wood (1912)	34
6=	Cy Young (1901)	33
=	Christy Mathewson (1904)	33
=	Walter Johnson (1912)	33
=	Grover Alexander (1916)	33
10=	Four players tied with	32

The only pitcher to win 30 games in a season since 1935 was Denny McLain of Detroit, who went 31–6 in 1968, a year in which pitchers dominated.

Most Walks Allowed in a Career

	PITCHER (SEASONS PLAYED)	WALKS
1	Nolan Ryan (1966–93)	2,795
2	Steve Carlton (1965–88)	1,833
3	Phil Niekro (1964–87)	1,809
4	Early Wynn (1939–63)	1,775
5	Bob Feller (1936–56)	1,764
6	Bobo Newsom (1929–53)	1,732
7	Amos Rusie (1889–1901)	1,707
8	Charlie Hough (1970–94)	1,665
9	Gus Weyhing (1887–1901)	1,570
10	Red Ruffing (1924–47)	1,541

For much of his career, Ryan was as well known for his wildness as his startling speed. He threw seven no-hitters, but never had a perfect game, thanks to walks.

Lowest Earned Run Average in a Season

	PITCHER (SEASON)	ERA
1	Tim Keefe (1880)	0.86
2	Dutch Leonard (1914)	0.96
3	Mordecai Brown (1906)	1.04
4	Bob Gibson (1968)	1.12
5	Christy Mathewson (1909)	1.14
6	Walter Johnson (1913)	1.14
7	Jack Pfiester (1907)	1.15
8	Addie Joss (1908)	1.16
9	Carl Lundgren (1907)	1.17
10	Denny Driscoll (1882)	1.21

Gibson's 1968 mark stands out as the lowest in recent years. That season was called the "Year of the Pitcher," when hitting stats were at an all-time low.

DID YOU KNOW?
Four balls equal a walk, right? Not until 1889, though. Before then, the number of balls for a walk (or base on balls) was as high as nine, before shrinking to today's number.

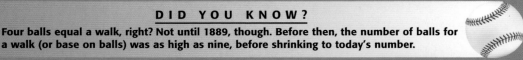

Top 10 Most Saves in a Season

Pitcher (Season)/Saves

1 **Bobby Thigpen** (1990), 57 **2** = **John Smoltz** (2002), 55; = **Eric Gagne** (2003), 55 **4** = **Randy Myers** (1993), 53; = **Trevor Hoffman** (1998), 53 **6** **Eric Gagne** (2002), 52 **7** = **Dennis Eckersley** (1992), 51; = **Rod Beck** (1998), 51 **9** **Mariano Rivera** (2001), 50 **10** = **Dennis Eckersley** (1990), 48; = **Rod Beck** (1993), 48; = **Jeff Shaw** (1998), 48

SUPER SAVER

In 18 seasons with eight teams, Lee Smith has nine seasons with 30 or more saves and led his league in saves four times.

Most Losses in a Career

	PITCHER (SEASONS PLAYED)	LOSSES
1	**Cy Young** (1890–1911)	316
2	**Jim Galvin** (1875–92)	308
3	**Nolan Ryan** (1966–93)	292
4	**Walter Johnson** (1907–27)	279
5	**Phil Niekro** (1964–87)	274
6	**Gaylord Perry** (1962–83)	265
7	**Don Sutton** (1966–88)	256
8	**Jack Powell** (1897–1912)	254
9	**Eppa Rixey** (1912–33)	251
10	**Bert Blyleven** (1970–92)	250

The old saying is that you've got to be pretty good to pitch long enough to lose this often. Notice that all-time "loser" Cy Young also holds the record for most career wins.

Most Games Pitched in a Season

	PITCHER (SEASON)	GAMES
1	**Mike Marshall** (1974)	106
2	**Kent Tekulve** (1979)	94
3	**Mike Marshall** (1973)	92
4	**Kent Tekulve** (1978)	91
5	=**Wayne Granger** (1969)	90
	=**Mike Marshall** (1979)	90
	=**Kent Tekulve** (1987)	90
8	=**Mark Eichhorn** (1987)	89
	=**Julian Tavarez** (1997)	89
	=**Steve Kline** (2001)	89
	=**Paul Quantrill** (2003)	89

Marshall was legendary for his fitness and preparation, and later wrote books on training and workouts for pitchers.

FIELDING ARTISTS

GOLD GLOVE

This photo is of Willie Mays's 1962 Rawlings Gold Glove. Since 1957, baseball writers have voted for the top fielders at each position. The size of this glove would be amazing to early fielders, who used tiny gloves or no gloves at all. The improvement in equipment and training in recent years has meant that many of the top all-time fielders played in recent seasons.

Career Fielding Average, First Base

	FIELDER (SEASONS PLAYED)	FIELDING AVERAGE
1	Steve Garvey (1969–87)	.996
2	Don Mattingly (1982–95)	.996
3	Wes Parker (1964–72)	.996
4	J.T. Snow* (1992–)	.995
5	Dan Driessen (1973–87)	.995
6	David Segui* (1990–)	.995
7	John Olerud* (1989–)	.995
8	Jim Spencer (1968–82)	.995
9	Tino Martinez* (1990–)	.995
10	Mark Grace* (1988–)	.995

Career Fielding Average, Second Base

	FIELDER (SEASONS PLAYED)	FIELDING AVERAGE
1	Ryne Sandberg (1981–97)	.989
2	Tom Herr (1979–91)	.989
3	Mickey Morandini (1990–2000)	.989
4	Jose Lind (1987–95)	.988
5	Jody Reed (1987–97)	.988
6	Bret Boone* (1992–)	.987
7	Jim Gantner (1976–92)	.985
8	Craig Biggio* (1988–)	.984
9	Frank White (1973–90)	.984
10	Bobby Grich (1970–86)	.984

Sandberg was not only the best fielder at his position, per this list, but he was also one of the top-hitting "keystone" men ever.

Career Fielding Average, Third Base

	FIELDER (SEASONS PLAYED)	FIELDING AVERAGE
1	Brooks Robinson (1955–77)	.971
2	Ken Reitz (1972–82)	.970
3	George Kell (1943–57)	.969
4	Steve Buechele (1985–95)	.968
5	Don Money (1968–83)	.968
6	Don Wert (1963–71)	.968
7	Willie Kamm (1923–35)	.967
8	Heinie Groh (1912–27)	.967
9	Carney Lansford (1978–92)	.966
10	Travis Fryman (1990–2002)	.965

Career Fielding Average, Shortstop

	FIELDER (SEASONS PLAYED)	FIELDING AVERAGE
1	Omar Vizquel* (1989–)	.983
2	Mike Bordick* (1990–)	.982
3	Larry Bowa (1970–85)	.980
4	Tony Fernandez (1983–2001)	.980
5	Cal Ripken, Jr. (1981–2001)	.979
6	Ozzie Smith (1978–96)	.978
7	Spike Owen (1983–95)	.977
8	Alan Trammell (1977–96)	.977
9	Mark Belanger (1965–82)	.977
10	Bucky Dent (1973–84)	.976

Career Fielding Average, Outfield

	FIELDER (SEASONS PLAYED)	FIELDING AVERAGE
1	Darryl Hamilton (1988–2001)	.995
2	Darren Lewis (1990–2002)	.994
3	Terry Puhl (1977–91)	.993
4	Brett Butler (1981–97)	.993
5	Pete Rose (1963–86)	.991
6	Amos Otis (1967–84)	.991
7	Joe Rudi (1967–82)	.991
8	Mickey Stanley (1964–78)	.991
9	Tom Goodwin (1991–)	.991
10	Robin Yount (1974–93)	.990

DID YOU KNOW?
Fielding average is calculated by adding putouts and assists and dividing that total by the total of putouts, assists, and errors. The fewer errors you make, the higher your average.

Career Fielding Average, Pitcher

FIELDER (SEASONS PLAYED)   FIELDING AVERAGE

	FIELDER (SEASONS PLAYED)	FIELDING AVERAGE
1	**Don Mossi** (1954–65)	.990
2	**Gary Nolan** (1967–77)	.990
3	**Rick Rhoden** (1974–89)	.989
4	**Lon Warneke** (1930–45)	.988
5	**Jim Wilson** (1945–58)	.988
6	**Woodie Fryman** (1966–83)	.988
7	**Larry Gura** (1970–85)	.986
8	**Mike Mussina*** (1991–)	.986
9	**Grover Alexander** (1911–30)	.985
10	**Alvin Crowder** (1926–36)	.984

A good-fielding pitcher can really help himself out by becoming a fifth infielder. Mussina is not only one of the A.L.'s top pitchers, he has won five Gold Gloves. Since ending his baseball career, Rhoden has become a professional golfer, winning consistently on a celebrity pro tour.

OH, MY, OMAR!

Cleveland's Omar Vizquel, the all-time fielding average leader for shortstops, specializes in making barehand grabs of hot liners, plays that leave fans and opponents in awe.

HUMAN VACUUM CLEANER

Baltimore third baseman Brooks Robinson set a new standard for excellence at the hot corner over his 23-year career. He almost singlehandedly won the 1970 World Series with several game-saving plays at third base, including this diving grab.

Career Fielding Average, Catcher

FIELDER (SEASONS PLAYED)   FIELDING AVERAGE

	FIELDER (SEASONS PLAYED)	FIELDING AVERAGE
1	**Bill Freehan** (1961–76)	.993
2	**Elston Howard** (1955–68)	.993
3	**Jim Sundberg** (1974–89)	.993
4	**Sherm Lollar** (1946–63)	.992
5	**Mike Macfarlane** (1987–99)	.992
6	**Johnny Edwards** (1961–74)	.992
7	**Tom Haller** (1961–72)	.992
8	**Lance Parrish** (1977–95)	.991
9	**Jerry Grote** (1963–81)	.991
10	**Ernie Whitt** (1976–91)	.991

* Active through 2003

GOLD GLOVES

The lists on these two pages show the ten most recent winners of the Rawlings Gold Glove award for each position. Gold Gloves are given to one player in each league at each infield position, while three awards are given in each league for outfielders. Individual awards for right-, center-, and leftfield are not given; all outfielders are lumped together. Players earn these awards by subjective voting, not by strict statistical measures.

GO AHEAD, TRY IT...

Ivan Rodrigue, has redefined the catching position with his remarkable throwing arm. Few baserunners even attempt to steal on him anymore, while runners on first need to be on their toes, since he's equally adept at pickoffs.

THE TOP 10

Most Recent Catchers

N.L. WINNER	YEAR	A.L. WINNER
Mike Matheny, St. Louis.	2003	**Bengie Molina**, Anaheim
Brad Ausmus, Houston	2002	**Bengie Molina**, Anaheim
Brad Ausmus, Houston	2001	**Ivan Rodriguez**, Texas
Mike Matheny, St. Louis	2000	**Ivan Rodriguez**, Texas
Mike Lieberthal, Phil.	1999	**Ivan Rodriguez**, Texas
Charles Johnson, Fla.-L.A.	1998	**Ivan Rodriguez**, Texas
Charles Johnson, Florida	1997	**Ivan Rodriguez**, Texas
Charles Johnson, Florida	1996	**Ivan Rodriguez**, Texas
Charles Johnson, Florida	1995	**Ivan Rodriguez**, Texas
Tom Pagnozzi, St. Louis	1994	**Ivan Rodriguez**, Texas

THE TOP 10

Most Recent First Basemen

N.L. WINNER	YEAR	A.L. WINNER
Derrek Lee, Florida	2003	**John Olerud**, Seattle
Todd Helton, Colorado	2002	**John Olerud**, Seattle
Todd Helton, Colorado	2001	**Doug Mientkiewicz**, Minn.
J.T. Snow, S.F.	2000	**John Olerud**, Seattle
J.T. Snow, S.F.	1999	**Rafael Palmeiro**, Texas
J.T. Snow, S.F.	1998	**Rafael Palmeiro**, Baltimore
J.T. Snow, S.F.	1997	**Rafael Palmeiro**, Baltimore
Mark Grace, Chicago	1996	**J.T. Snow**, California
Mark Grace, Chicago	1995	**J.T. Snow**, California
Jeff Bagwell, Houston	1994	**Don Mattingly**, New York

THE TOP 10

Most Recent Pitchers

N.L. WINNER	YEAR	A.L. WINNER
Mike Hampton, Atlanta	2003	**Mike Mussina**, New York
Greg Maddux, Atlanta	2002	**Kenny Rogers**, Texas
Greg Maddux, Atlanta	2001	**Mike Mussina**, New York
Greg Maddux, Atlanta	2000	**Kenny Rogers**, Texas
Greg Maddux, Atlanta	1999	**Mike Mussina**, Baltimore
Greg Maddux, Atlanta	1998	**Mike Mussina**, Baltimore
Greg Maddux, Atlanta	1997	**Mike Mussina**, Baltimore
Greg Maddux, Atlanta	1996	**Mike Mussina**, Baltimore
Greg Maddux, Atlanta	1995	**Mark Langston**, California
Greg Maddux, Atlanta	1994	**Mark Langston**, California

THE TOP 10

Most Recent Second Basemen

N.L. WINNER	YEAR	A.L. WINNER
Luis Castillo, Florida	2003	**Bret Boone**, Seattle
Fernando Viña, St. Louis	2002	**Bret Boone**, Seattle
Fernando Viña, St. Louis	2001	**Roberto Alomar**, Cleveland
Pokey Reese, Cincinnati	2000	**Roberto Alomar**, Cleveland
Pokey Reese, Cincinnati	1999	**Roberto Alomar**, Cleveland
Bret Boone, Cincinnati	1998	**Roberto Alomar**, Baltimore
Craig Biggio, Houston	1997	**Chuck Knoblauch**, Minnesota
Craig Biggio, Houston	1996	**Roberto Alomar**, Toronto
Craig Biggio, Houston	1995	**Roberto Alomar**, Toronto
Craig Biggio, Houston	1994	**Roberto Alomar**, Toronto

QUIZ TIME

What rare Gold Glove feat did outfielder Jim Edmonds accomplish in 2000? Hint: In 2000, he joined the St. Louis Cardinals. (Answer on page 26.)

THE TOP 10

Most Recent Third Basemen

N.L. WINNER	YEAR	A.L. WINNER
Scott Rolen, St. Louis	**2003**	**Eric Chavez**, Oakland
Scott Rolen, Phil./St. Louis	**2002**	**Eric Chavez**, Oakland
Scott Rolen, Philadelphia	**2001**	**Eric Chavez**, Oakland
Scott Rolen, Philadelphia	**2000**	**Travis Fryman**, Cleveland
Robin Ventura, New York	**1999**	**Scott Brosius**, New York
Scott Rolen, Philadelphia	**1998**	**Robin Ventura**, Chicago
Ken Caminiti, San Diego	**1997**	**Matt Williams**, Cleveland
Ken Caminiti, San Diego	**1996**	**Robin Ventura**, Chicago
Ken Caminiti, San Diego	**1995**	**Wade Boggs**, New York
Matt Williams, S.F.	**1994**	**Wade Boggs**, New York

THE TOP 10

Most Recent Shortstops

N.L. WINNER	YEAR	A.L. WINNER
Edgar Renteria, St. Louis	**2003**	**Alex Rodriguez**, Texas
Edgar Renteria, St. Louis	**2002**	**Alex Rodriguez**, Texas
Orlando Cabrera, Montreal	**2001**	**Omar Vizquel**, Cleveland
Neifi Perez, Colorado	**2000**	**Omar Vizquel**, Cleveland
Rey Ordoñez, New York	**1999**	**Omar Vizquel**, Cleveland
Rey Ordoñez, New York	**1998**	**Omar Vizquel**, Cleveland
Rey Ordoñez, New York	**1997**	**Omar Vizquel**, Cleveland
Barry Larkin, Cincinnati	**1996**	**Omar Vizquel**, Cleveland
Barry Larkin, Cincinnati	**1995**	**Omar Vizquel**, Cleveland
Barry Larkin, Cincinnati	**1994**	**Omar Vizquel**, Cleveland

THE TOP 10

Most Recent Outfielders

N.L. WINNERS	YEAR	A.L. WINNERS
Andruw Jones, Atlanta **Jim Edmonds**, St. Louis **Jose Cruz**, S.F.	**2003**	**Ichiro Suzuki**, Seattle **Torii Hunter**, Minnesota **Mike Cameron**, Seattle
Larry Walker, Colorado **Andruw Jones**, Atlanta **Jim Edmonds**, St. Louis	**2003**	**Darin Erstad**, Anaheim **Ichiro Suzuki**, Seattle **Torii Hunter**, Minnesota
Andruw Jones, Atlanta **Larry Walker**, Colorado **Jim Edmonds**, St. Louis	**2001**	**Ichiro Suzuki**, Seattle **Mike Cameron**, Seattle **Torii Hunter**, Minnesota
Andruw Jones, Atlanta **Steve Finley**, Arizona **Jim Edmonds**, St. Louis	**2000**	**Darin Erstad**, Anaheim **Bernie Williams**, New York **Jermaine Dye**, Kansas City
Andruw Jones, Atlanta **Steve Finley**, Arizona **Larry Walker**, Colorado	**1999**	**Ken Griffey, Jr.**, Seattle **Shawn Green**, Toronto **Bernie Williams**, New York
Barry Bonds, S.F. **Andruw Jones**, Atlanta **Larry Walker**, Colorado	**1998**	**Jim Edmonds**, Anaheim **Ken Griffey, Jr.**, Seattle **Bernie Williams**, New York
Barry Bonds, S.F. **Raul Mondesi**, Los Angeles **Larry Walker**, Colorado	**1997**	**Jim Edmonds**, Anaheim **Ken Griffey, Jr.**, Seattle **Bernie Williams**, New York
Barry Bonds, S.F. **Marquis Grissom**, Atlanta **Steve Finley**, San Diego	**1996**	**Ken Griffey, Jr.**, Seattle **Kenny Lofton**, Cleveland **Jay Buhner**, Seattle
Barry Bonds, S.F. **Marquis Grissom**, Atlanta **Steve Finley**, San Diego	**1995**	**Ken Griffey, Jr.**, Seattle **Kenny Lofton**, Cleveland **Devon White**, Toronto
Barry Bonds, S.F. **Darren Lewis**, S.F. **Marquis Grissom**, Montreal	**1994**	**Ken Griffey, Jr.**, Seattle **Devon White**, Toronto **Kenny Lofton**, Cleveland

YOUNG GLOVE

Atlanta centerfielder Andruw Jones is not only the second Major Leaguer from Curaçao, but he's one of the top young fielders in the game.

GOLD GLOVES

Most Gold Gloves, Pitcher

PITCHER	GOLD GLOVES
1 Jim Kaat	16
2 Greg Maddux*	13
3 Bob Gibson	9
4 Bobby Shantz	8
5 Mark Langston	7
6= Phil Niekro	6
= Ron Guidry	6
= Mike Mussina*	6
9 Jim Palmer	4
10 Harvey Haddix	3

Although he was 6'4" and weighed more than 200 pounds, Jim "Kitty" Kaat (pronounced "KAHT") is generally regarded as the best-fielding pitcher ever. His 16 Gold Gloves attest to that. But he was a pretty fair pitcher, too, winning 283 games in his career with a lifetime 3.45 ERA.

Most Gold Gloves, Catcher

CATCHER	GOLD GLOVES
1= Johnny Bench	10
= Ivan Rodriguez*	10
3 Bob Boone	7
4 Jim Sundberg	6
5 Bill Freehan	5
6= Del Crandall	4
= Charles Johnson*	4
= Tony Peña	4
9= Seven players tied with	3

"THE CATCH"

To make the most famous catch in baseball history, Willie Mays had to track down Vic Wertz's drive on a dead run and with his back to the plate. The catch came, dramatically, in Game 1 of the 1954 World Series.

Most Gold Gloves, First Base

FIRST BASEMAN	GOLD GLOVES
1 Keith Hernandez	11
2 Don Mattingly	9
3 George Scott	8
4= Vic Power	7
= Bill White	7
6= Wes Parker	6
= J.T. Snow*	6
8= Steve Garvey	4
= Mark Grace*	4
10= Five players tied with	3

Most Gold Gloves, Second Base

SECOND BASEMAN	GOLD GLOVES
1= Roberto Alomar*	10
2 Ryne Sandberg	9
3= Bill Mazeroski	8
= Frank White	8
5= Joe Morgan	5
= Bobby Richardson	5
7= Craig Biggio*	4
= Bobby Grich	4
9= Seven players tied with	3

DID YOU KNOW?

In 1957, Gold Gloves were given to one player from each outfield position: Willie Mays in center, Al Kaline in right, and Minnie Minoso in left.

THE TOP 10

Most Gold Gloves, Third Base

THIRD BASEMAN	GOLD GLOVES
1 Brooks Robinson	16
2 Mike Schmidt	10
3= Buddy Bell	6
= Robin Ventura*	6
5= Ken Boyer	5
= Doug Rader	5
= Ron Santo	5
= Scott Rolen*	5
9= Gary Gaetti	4
= Matt Williams*	4

THE TOP 10

Most Gold Gloves, Shortstop

SHORTSTOP	GOLD GLOVES
1 Ozzie Smith	13
2 Luis Aparicio	9
= Omar Vizquel*	9
4= Mark Belanger	8
5 Dave Concepcion	5
6= Tony Fernandez	4
= Alan Trammell	4
8= Barry Larkin*	3
= Roy McMillan	3
= Rey Ordoñez*	3

The Wizard of Oz set the standard for shortstops during his 19-year career with the Padres and Cardinals. Current Indians shortstop Omar Vizquel might be approaching Ozzie's status, however.

THE TOP 10

Most Gold Gloves, Outfield

OUTFIELDER	GOLD GLOVES
1= Roberto Clemente	12
= Willie Mays	12
3= Ken Griffey, Jr.*	10
= Al Kaline	10
5= Paul Blair	8
= Barry Bonds*	8
= Andre Dawson	8
= Dwight Evans	8
= Garry Maddox	8
10= Jim Edmonds*	7
= Curt Flood	7
= Devon White	7
= Dave Winfield	7
= Carl Yastrzemski	7

THE TOP 10

Most Consecutive Gold Gloves, Any Position

PLAYER, POSITION	CONSEC. GGs
1= Jim Kaat, P	16
= Brooks Robinson, 3B	16
3= Ozzie Smith, SS	13
= Greg Maddux*, P	13
5= Willie Mays, OF	12
= Roberto Clemente, OF	12
7 Keith Hernandez, 1B	11
8= Johnny Bench, C	10
= Ivan Rodriguez*, C	10
= Ken Griffey, Jr.*, OF	10

Bob Gibson, P, Ryne Sandberg, 2B and Omar Vizquel*, SS have each won 9 consecutive Gold Gloves.

Active through 2003

ASSISTS AND PUTOUTS

Top 10 Career Assists, Third Base
Player/Assists

1 **Brooks Robinson**, 6,205 **2** **Graig Nettles**, 5,279
3 **Mike Schmidt**, 5,045 **4** **Buddy Bell**, 4,925
5 **Ron Santo**, 4,581 **6** **Gary Gaetti**, 4,531
7 **Eddie Mathews**, 4,322 **8** **Wade Boggs**, 4,246
9 **Aurelio Rodriguez**, 4,150 **10** **Ron Cey**, 4,018

Top 10 Most Assists in a Season, Third Base
Player (Season) Assists

1 **Graig Nettles** (1971) 412 **2** = **Graig Nettles** (1973) 410; =
Brooks Robinson (1974) 410 **4** = **Harlond Clift** (1937) 405;
= **Brooks Robinson** (1967) 405 **6** **Mike Schmidt** (1974) 404
7 **Doug DeCinces** (1982) 399 **8** = **Clete Boyer** (1962) 396;
= **Mike Schmidt** (1977) 396; = **Buddy Bell** (1982) 396

RIFLE-ARMED ROBERTO

Pittsburgh Pirates rightfielder Roberto Clemente remains the standard by which outfield arms are judged. The Puerto Rico native was one of the first Hispanic superstars, showing his talents at the plate with a pair of batting titles, on the bases with an all-out running style, and in the field with a rifle arm that probably has not been equalled. Clemente won 12 Gold Gloves and led the National League in assists a record five times. In the 1971 World Series, he batted .414, but he also made 15 putouts and made a throw to nail a runner at first that remains one of the best defensive plays in World Series history. He was named the MVP of the Series, which the Pirates won. On the final day of 1972, he was killed in a plane crash while delivering relief supplies to victims of an earthquake in Nicaragua.

SNAP SHOTS

THE TOP 10
Most Career Assists, Shortstop

	PLAYER (SEASONS PLAYED)	ASSISTS
1	**Ozzie Smith** (1978–96)	8,375
2	**Luis Aparicio** (1956–73)	8,016
3	**Bill Dahlen** (1891–1911)	7,505
4	**Rabbit Maranville** (1912–35)	7,354
5	**Luke Appling** (1930–50)	7,218
6	**Tommy Corcoran** (1890–1907)	7,110
7	**Cal Ripken, Jr.*** (1981–)	6,977
8	**Larry Bowa** (1970–85)	6,857
9	**Dave Concepcion** (1970–88)	6,594
10	**Dave Bancroft** (1915–30)	6,561

THE TOP 10
Most Career Assists, Catcher

	PLAYER (SEASONS PLAYED)	ASSISTS
1	**Deacon McGuire** (1884–1912)	1,860
2	**Ray Schalk** (1912–29)	1,811
3	**Steve O'Neill** (1911–28)	1,698
4	**Red Dooin** (1902–16)	1,590
5	**Chief Zimmer** (1884–1903)	1,580
6	**Johnny Kling** (1900–13)	1,554
7	**Ivey Wingo** (1911–29)	1,487
8	**Wilbert Robinson** (1886–1902)	1,454
9	**Bill Bergen** (1901–11)	1,444
10	**Wally Schang** (1913–31)	1,420

THE TOP 10
Most Assists in a Season, Catcher

	PLAYER (SEASON)	ASSISTS
1	**Bill Rariden** (1915)	238
2	**Bill Rariden** (1914)	215
3	**Pat Moran** (1903)	214
4	= **Oscar Stanage** (1911)	212
	= **Art Wilson** (1914)	212
6	**Gabby Street** (1909)	210
7	**Frank Snyder** (1915)	204
8	**George Gibson** (1910)	203
9	= **Bill Bergen** (1909)	202
	= **Claude Berry** (1914)	202

THE TOP 10
Most Assists in a Season, Shortstop

	PLAYER (SEASON)	ASSISTS
1	**Ozzie Smith** (1980)	621
2	**Glenn Wright** (1924)	601
3	**Dave Bancroft** (1920)	598
4	**Tommy Thevenow** (1926)	597
5	**Ivan DeJesus** (1977)	595
6	**Cal Ripken** (1984)	583
7	**Whitey Wietelmann** (1943)	581
8	**Dave Bancroft** (1922)	579
9	**Rabbit Maranville** (1914)	574
10	**Don Kessinger** (1968)	573

* Active through 2003

DID YOU KNOW?
Putout: When a player tags the base or the player to make an out. Assist: A throw to a player who makes a putout. (Page 22 answer: Edmonds won Gold Gloves in both leagues.)

THE TOP 10

Most Career Assists, Second Base

	PLAYER (SEASONS PLAYED)	ASSISTS
1	**Eddie Collins** (1906–30)	7,630
2	**Charlie Gehringer** (1924–42)	7,068
3	**Joe Morgan** (1963–84)	6,967
4	**Bid McPhee** (1882–99)	6,915
5	**Bill Mazeroski** (1956–72)	6,685
6	**Lou Whitaker** (1977–95)	6,653
7	**Nellie Fox** (1947–65)	6,373
8	**Ryne Sandberg** (1981–97)	6,363
9	**Willie Randolph** (1975–92)	6,336
10	**Napoleon Lajoie** (1896–1916)	6,262

BILLY BUCKS

Though unfortunately remembered for an error in Game 6 of the seven-game 1986 World Series, Bill Buckner was one of the game's top-fielding first basemen throughout his career.

Most Assists in a Season, Second Base

	PLAYER (SEASON)	ASSISTS
1	**Frankie Frisch** (1927)	641
2	**Hughie Critz** (1926)	588
3	**Rogers Hornsby** (1927)	582
4	**Ski Melillo** (1930)	572
5	**Ryne Sandberg** (1983)	571
6	**Rabbit Maranville** (1924)	568
7	**Frank Parkinson** (1922)	562
8	**Tony Cuccinello** (1936)	559
9	**Johnny Hodapp** (1930)	557
10	**Lou Bierbauer** (1892)	555

Most Career Assists, First Base

	PLAYER (SEASONS PLAYED)	ASSISTS
1	**Eddie Murray** (1977–97)	1,865
2	**Keith Hernandez** (1974–90)	1,682
3	**Mark Grace*** (1988–)	1,601
4	**George Sisler** (1915–30)	1,529
5	**Wally Joyner** (1986–00)	1,452
6	**Mickey Vernon** (1939–60)	1,448
7	**Fred Tenney** (1894–11)	1,363
8=	**Bill Buckner** (1969–90)	1,351
=	**Chris Chambliss** (1971–88)	1,351
10	**Norm Cash** (1958–74)	1,317

First basemen who put up good assists numbers are generally the better fielders. A first baseman who can contribute in ways other than just catching infielders' throws can significantly improve a team's defense.

Most Assists in a Season, First Base

	PLAYER (SEASON)	ASSISTS
1	**Jiggs Donahue** (1907)	1,846
2	**George Kelly** (1920)	1,759
3	**Phil Todt** (1926)	1,755
4	**Wally Pipp** (1926)	1,710
5	**Jiggs Donahue** (1906)	1,697
6	**Candy LaChance** (1904)	1,691
7	**Tom Jones** (1907)	1,687
8	**Ernie Banks** (1965)	1,682
9	**Wally Pipp** (1922)	1,667
10	**Lou Gehrig** (1927)	1,662

First basemen don't rack up as many assists as other fielders. Their main job is cleanly catching throws from infielders to make outs at first base. They also earn putouts by catching ground balls and tagging first base, or by catching fly balls or line drives.

MISCELLANEOUS STATS

Grounded into Most Double Plays

PLAYER (SEASONS PLAYED)	GIDPS
1 Cal Ripken, Jr. (1981–2001)	350
2 Hank Aaron (1954–76)	328
3 Carl Yastrzemski (1960–83)	323
4 Dave Winfield (1974–89)	319
5 Eddie Murray (1977–97)	316
6 Jim Rice (1974–89)	315
7 Harold Baines (1980–2001)	298
8=Rusty Staub (1963–85)	297
=Brooks Robinson (1955–77)	297
10 Ted Simmons (1968–88)	287

This list is dominated by slow, righthanded sluggers who often pulled the ball.

Most Recent Unassisted Triple Plays

PLAYER, POSITION	YEAR
1 Rafael Furcal*, SS	2003
2 Randy Velarde, 2B	2000
3 John Valentin, SS	1994
4 Mickey Morandini, 2B	1992
5 Ron Hansen, SS	1968
6 Johnny Neun, 1B	1927
7 Jimmy Cooney, SS	1927
8 Glenn Wright, SS	1925
9 Ernie Padgett, SS	1923
10 George Burns, 1B	1923

A fielder making three putouts by himself on one batted ball is the rarest fielding feat.

Most Batters Hit by a Pitcher

PITCHER	HBPs
1 Gus Weyhing	278
2 Chick Fraser	219
3 Pink Hawley	210
4 Walter Johnson	205
5 Eddie Plank	190
6 Tony Mullane	185
7 Joe McGinnity	179
8 Charlie Hough	174
9 Clark Griffith	171
10 Cy Young	163

With one of the best fastballs of all time, Walter Johnson had a fearsome weapon to use. He also wasn't afraid to throw inside, and not everyone got out of the way.

MY THREE VICTIMS

Another famous triple play occured during the 1920 World Series. Here, Indians second baseman Bill Wambsganss, left, poses with the three men he put out in one play: Clarence Mitchell, Pete Kilduff, and Otto Miller.

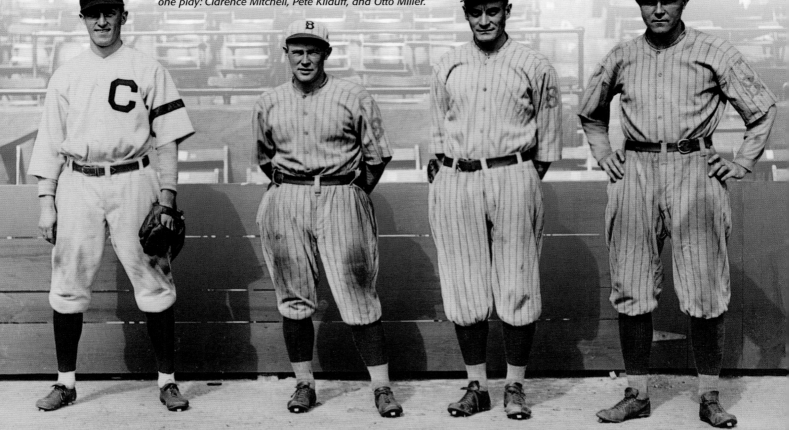

THE TOP 10

Best 2B/SS Double-Play Combination in a Season

	YEAR, 2ND BASEMAN/SHORTSTOP (DPS), TEAM	TOTAL DPS
1	1966, **Bill Mazeroski** (161), **Gene Alley** (128), Pitt.	289
2	1950, **Gerry Priddy** (150), **Johnny Lipon** (126), Det.	276
3	1962, **Bill Mazeroski** (138), **Dick Groat** (126), Pitt.	264
4	1949, **Bobby Doerr** (134), **Vern Stephens** (128), Bos.	262
5	1961, **Bill Mazeroski** (144), **Dick Groat** (117), Pitt.	261
6=	1950, **Jerry Coleman** (137), **Phil Rizzuto** (123), NYY	260
=	1966, **Bobby Knoop** (135), **Jim Fregosi** (125), Cal.	260
8	1928, **Hughie Critz** (124), **Hod Ford** (128), Cin.	252
9	1954, **Johnny Temple** (117), **Roy McMillan** (129), Cin.	246
10=	1943, **Ray Mack** (123), **Lou Boudreau** (122), Cleve.	245
=	1950, **Bobby Doerr** (130), **Vern Stephens** (115), Bos.	245
=	1958, **Bill Mazeroski** (118), **Dick Groat** (127), Pitt.	245
=	1974, **Dave Cash** (141), **Larry Bowa** (104), Phi.	245

When he was inducted into the Baseball Hall of Fame in 2001, Bill Mazeroski thanked voters for recognizing defense. "Maz" earned his selection mostly on the strength of his great glove.

PHILADELPHIA FLINGER
Robin Roberts of the Phillies enjoys a place in the Hall of Fame, but he doesn't enjoy his all-time record for most home runs allowed.

THE TOP 10

Most Times Hit by Pitch, Career

	PITCHER	HBPs
1	**Hughie Jennings**	287
2	**Tommy Tucker**	272
3	**Don Baylor**	267
4	**Ron Hunt**	243
5	**Craig Biggio***	241
6	**Dan McGann**	230
7	**Frank Robinson**	198
8	**Minnie Miñoso**	192
9	**Jake Beckley**	183
10	**Andres Galarraga***	177

Until he was overtaken by power-hitting Don Baylor, Expos infielder Ron Hunt set the modern standard for being plunked by pitches. In 1971, Hunt was hit by pitches 50 times, the most ever since 1900.

THE TOP 10

Most Home Runs Allowed, Single-season

	PITCHER, SEASON	HRS
1	**Bert Blyleven**, 1986	50
2	**Jose Lima***, 2000	48
3=	**Robin Roberts**, 1956	46
=	**Bert Blyleven**, 1987	46
5	**Pedro Ramos**, 1957	43
6	**Denny McLain**, 1966	42
7	**Robin Roberts**, 1955	41
=	**Phil Niekro**, 1979	41
=	**Rick Helling**, 1999	41
10	Nine tied with	40

Blyleven must have been doing something right between giving up all those dingers. In 1986, he also won 17 games for the Twins.

THE TOP 10

Most Career Home Runs Allowed

	PITCHER	HRS
1	**Robin Roberts**	505
2	**Ferguson Jenkins**	484
3	**Phil Niekro**	482
4	**Don Sutton**	472
5	**Frank Tanana**	448
6	**Warren Spahn**	434
7	**Bert Blyleven**	430
8	**Steve Carlton**	414
9	**Gaylord Perry**	399
10	**Jim Kaat**	395

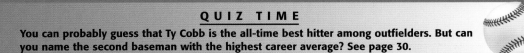

QUIZ TIME

You can probably guess that Ty Cobb is the all-time best hitter among outfielders. But can you name the second baseman with the highest career average? See page 30.

29

HISTORY'S BEST

All-Time Hitters, Pitchers

PITCHERS	CAREER BATTING AVERAGE
1 Babe Ruth	.299
2 Guy Hecker	.297
3 Jack Stivetts	.295
4 Jim Devlin	.293
5 Charlie Ferguson	.288
6 George Uhle	.286
7 Wes Ferrell	.284
8 Charlie Sweeney	.284
9 Cy Seymour	.280
10 Doc Crandall	.279

Before the designated hitter came along in the American League in 1973, all pitchers took their regular turns at bat. In the National League, they still do. Pitchers rarely are great hitters; they don't practice hitting often and they only play every four or five days. However, many are good athletes who may have batted more often when younger.

THE RAJAH
Cardinals second baseman Rogers Hornsby batted .424 in 1922, the second-highest of the century. No player has topped that mark since.

All-Time Hitters, Shortstops

PLAYER	CAREER BATTING AVERAGE
1 Honus Wagner	.328
2 Arky Vaughan	.318
3 Joe Sewell	.312
4 Luke Appling	.310
5 Ed McKean	.308
6 Joe Cronin	.301
7 Barry Larkin	.299
8 Lou Boudreau	.295
9 George Davis	.295
10 Jack Glasscock	.294

All-Time Hitters, First Basemen

PLAYER	CAREER BATTING AVERAGE
1 Dan Brouthers	.349
2 Bill Terry	.341
3 George Sisler	.340
4 Lou Gehrig	.340
5 Cap Anson	.333
6 Rod Carew	.328
7 Jimmie Foxx	.325
8 Roger Connor	.323
9 Hank Greenberg	.313
10 Frank Thomas*	.310

"Big" Dan Brouthers won five batting titles in his career, which stretched from 1879–1896. He was also one of baseball's early sluggers, with a .519 career slugging average that was the highest of any player in the 19th century.

All-Time Hitters, Second Basemen

PLAYER	CAREER BATTING AVERAGE
1 Rogers Hornsby	.358
2 Nap Lajoie	.338
3 Eddie Collins	.333
4 Charlie Gehringer	.320
5 Frankie Frisch	.316
6 Jackie Robinson	.311
7 Cupid Childs	.306
8 Billy Herman	.304
9 Buddy Myer	.303
10 Roberto Alomar*	.301

Lajoie hit over .300 in 16 of his 21 seasons and his .426 average in 1901 is the highest ever in the American League. Along with his skills as batter, Eddie Collins led his league in fielding nine times, plus twice stole a record six bases in one game.

All-Time Hitters, Third Basemen

PLAYER	CAREER BATTING AVERAGE
1 Wade Boggs	.328
2 Pie Traynor	.320
3 Denny Lyons	.318
4 Frank Baker	.307
5 George Kell	.306
6 George Brett	.305
7 Bill Madlock	.305
8 Stan Hack	.301
9 Pinky Whitney	.295
10 Kevin Seitzer	.295

Boggs and catcher Mike Piazza are the only recent player atop one of these positional lists. Boggs batted above .300 14 times and had at least 200 hits in seven seasons. He rarely hit for power but was one of baseball's consistently successful hitters.

QUIZ TIME
What fireballing righthander received the most votes of any pitcher in 1999 balloting for Major League Baseball's All-Century Team? (See page 33.)

All-Time Hitters, Catchers

	PLAYER	CAREER BATTING AVERAGE
1	**Mickey Cochrane**	.320
2	**Mike Piazza***	.319
3	**Bill Dickey**	.313
4	**Spud Davis**	.308
5	**Ernie Lombardi**	.306
6	**Ivan Rodriguez***	.304
7	**Gabby Hartnett**	.297
8	**Manny Sanguillen**	.296
9	**Smoky Burgess**	.295
10	**Thurman Munson**	.292

AS EASY AS PIAZZA PIE

In his 11 big-league seasons, Mike Piazza has put up better numbers for home runs and RBIs (and is second in average) than most catchers in the Hall of Fame. He is the best hitter ever to play baseball's most demanding position.

All-Time Hitters, Outfielders

	PLAYER	CAREER BATTING AVERAGE
1	**Ty Cobb**	.366
2	**Joe Jackson**	.356
3	**Ed Delahanty**	.346
4	**Tris Speaker**	.345
5	**Billy Hamilton**	.344
6	**Ted Williams**	.344
7	**Babe Ruth**	.342
8	**Harry Heilmann**	.342
9	**Willie Keeler**	.341
10	**Tony Gwynn**	.338

History's Best

A CLASSY CLASS
A gathering of greats in 1939: (top) Honus Wagner, Pete Alexander, Tris Speaker, Nap Lajoie, George Sisler, Walter Johnson; (bottom) Eddie Collins, Babe Ruth, Connie Mack, Cy Young.

THE TOP 10

Most Hall-of-Fame Votes Received

	PLAYER	VOTES
1	Nolan Ryan	491
2	George Brett	488
3	Mike Schmidt	444
4	Steve Carlton	436
5	Dave Winfield	435
6	Ozzie Smith	433
7	Johnny Bench	431
8	Tom Seaver	425
9=	Kirby Puckett	423
=	Carl Yastrzemski	423
=	Eddie Murray	423

THE TOP 10

First 10 Negro League Players in the Hall of Fame

	PLAYER/POSITION	YEAR ELECTED
1	Satchel Paige/Pitcher	1971
2=	Josh Gibson/Catcher	1972
=	Buck Leonard/First Base	1972
4	Monte Irvin/Outfield	1973
5	Cool Papa Bell/Outfield	1974
6	Judy Johnson/Third Base	1975
7	Oscar Charleston/Outfield	1976
8=	Martin Dihigo/Pitcher-Outfield	1977
=	Pop Lloyd/Shortstop-First Base	1977
10	Rube Foster/Pitcher-Manager	1982

To make up for the past injustices that kept black ballplayers out of the Major Leagues, a special commission was set up in 1971 to select players from the Negro Leagues deemed worthy of induction in the Hall based on their career skills and achievements. The committee inducted nine players and disbanded in 1977. Through 2001, a total of 24 players from Negro League teams have been inducted.

The First 10 Players Elected to the Hall of Fame

Players/Year Elected

① Ty Cobb, Babe Ruth, Honus Wagner, Christy Mathewson, Walter Johnson, 1936 **②** Nap Lajoie, Tris Speaker, Cy Young, George Wright, 1937 **③** Grover Alexander, George Sisler, Eddie Collins, Willie Keeler, 1939

Okay, twelve. So sue us. These were the members of the first three player classes elected to the Baseball Hall of Fame. In addition, the following non-players were elected in these first three years: Managers John McGraw and Connie Mack, executives Ban Johnson and Morgan Bulkeley, and innovators Alexander Cartwright and Henry Chadwick.

THE TOP 10

Most Recent Hall-of-Fame Classes

YEAR	INDUCTEES
2003	Gary Carter, Eddie Murray
2002	Ozzie Smith
2001	Kirby Puckett, Dave Winfield, Bill Mazeroski, Hilton Smith
2000	Sparky Anderson, Carlton Fisk, Bid McPhee, Tony Perez, Turkey Stearnes
1999	George Brett, Orlando Cepeda, Nestor Chylak, Nolan Ryan, Frank Selee, Smokey Joe Williams, Robin Yount
1998	George Davis, Larry Doby, Lee McPhail, Joe Rogan, Don Sutton
1997	Nellie Fox, Tom Lasorda, Phil Niekro, Willie Wells
1996	Jim Bunning, Bill Foster, Ned Hanlon, Earl Weaver
1995	Richie Ashburn, Leon Day, William Hulbert, Mike Schmidt, Vic Willis
1994	Steve Carlton, Leo Durocher, Phil Rizzuto

New members of the Hall are announced each January, with induction ceremonies held at Cooperstown, New York, each July or August.

QUIZ TIME
Which of the great Negro League Hall of Famers listed here is the all-time leader in Negro League batting average? Hint: He didn't play in the outfield. See page 34 for the answer.

THE TOP 10

Highest Percentages of Hall of Fame Votes Received

PLAYER (INDUCTION YEAR)	PCT.
1 **Tom Seaver** (1992)	98.84
2 **Nolan Ryan** (1999)	98.79
3 **Ty Cobb** (1936)	98.20
4 **George Brett** (1999)	98.19
5 **Hank Aaron** (1982)	97.80
6 **Mike Schmidt** (1995)	96.52
7= **Johnny Bench** (1989)	96.40
= **Steve Carlton** (1994)	95.82
9= **Honus Wagner** (1936)	95.10
= **Babe Ruth** (1936)	95.10

Most members of the Baseball Hall of Fame are selected by the Baseball Writers Association of America's special panel of electors. In addition, there are special committees to elect players who played more than 15 years ago (Veterans' Committee), Negro League players, executives, and others. A person must be named on 75 percent of the ballots of his electors to be inducted; electors may select more than one player per year.

THE TOP 10

All-Century Team Most Votes, Fan Ballots

PLAYER, POSITION	VOTES
1 Lou Gehrig, 1B	1,207,992
2 Babe Ruth, OF	1,158,044
3 Henry Aaron, OF	1,156,782
4 Ted Williams, OF	1,125,583
5 Willie Mays, OF	1,115,896
6 Joe DiMaggio, OF	1,054,423
7 Johnny Bench, C	1,010,403
8 Nolan Ryan, RHP	992,040
9 Mickey Mantle, OF	988,168
10 Sandy Koufax, LHP	970,434

In 1999, fans and baseball experts selected the 30-member All-Century Team to honor the greatest players in baseball history. Two players were chosen at every infield position, along with nine pitchers and nine outfielders. These players received the highest numbers of total votes.

JUST PERFECT

Sandy Koufax, a member of MLB's All-Century team, is congratulated by teammates following his 1965 perfect game.

WHY COOPERSTOWN?
Why is the Baseball Hall of Fame in Cooperstown, New York? Good question. In 1905, sporting goods magnate Albert Spalding tried to find out who had "invented" baseball. A letter claimed that Union Army General Abner Doubleday "invented" baseball there one day in 1839. One problem: Doubleday didn't invent baseball. Nevertheless, the little town became the "home" of the game, and the Hall was opened there in 1939. Scholars have since agreed that baseball didn't have a single "inventor." **SNAP SHOTS**

THE TOP 10

Most Memorable Moments

1 Cal Ripken breaks Lou Gehrig's streak consecutive game streak (1995).

2 Hank Aaron breaks Babe Ruth's all-time home run record (1974).

3 Jackie Robinson becomes the first African-American since 1884 to play in the major leagues (1947).

4 Mark McGwire and Sammy Sosa* single-season home run record (1998).

5 Lou Gehrig retires, giving a famous farewell speech (1939).

6 Pete Rose passes Ty Cobb as the all-time hits leader (1985).

7 Ted Williams is the last man to bat above .400 (.406 in 1941).

8 Joe DiMaggio hits in 56 straight games (1941).

9 Kirk Gibson's pinch-hit home run in Game 1 sends the Dodgers on their way to a World Series upset (1988).

10 Nolan Ryan pitches his seventh career no-hitter (1991).

* Active through 2003

OL' SATCH

How good was Satchel Paige? According to legend, he would often send his fielders to the dugout during exhibition games…and then strike out the side.

THE TOP 10
All-Time Negro League Pitchers

	PLAYER	WINS
1	**Satchel Paige**	143
2	**Joe Rogan**	109
3	**Nip Winters**	89
4	**Bill Drake**	83
5	**Bill Foster**	79
6	**Webster McDonald**	65
7	**Chet Brewer**	51
8	**Ted Radcliffe**	49

Holway's book lists only the top eight pitchers, ranked by pitching wins. These career numbers might seem low in comparison to Major League totals, but the Negro League season was shorter, and organized leagues were not around for as many years. However, all these pitchers played in many exhibition games along with organized league games. Ted "Double Duty" Radcliffe gained fame and a great nickname by pitching one end of a doubleheader and catching the other.

The Top Ten All-Time Negro League Batters
Player/Batting Average

1 Josh Gibson, .379 **2 Chino Smith**, .375 **3 Jud Wilson**, .370 **4** = **Dobie Moore**, .359; = **Dewey Creacy**, .359 **6 Willie Wells**, .358 **7** = **Oscar Charleston**, .353; = **Valentin Dreke**, .353 **9 Turkey Stearnes**, .352 **10 Cool Papa Bell**, .343

Negro League stats are famously incomplete and hard to track down. Thanks to John Holway's "Blackball Stars" for these Negro League historical lists.

POWER MAN

Slugging catcher Josh Gibson was, according to some, the greatest hitter of all time in any league. Some historians credit him with more homers than Ruth or Aaron.

THE TOP 10
Federal League Teams

	TEAM	TOTAL PCT.
1	**Indianapolis***	.575
2	**Chicago**	.560
3	**Newark***	.526
4	**Pittsburgh**	.495
5	**Buffalo**	.493
6	**St. Louis**	.488
7	**Kansas City**	.486
8	**Brooklyn**	.480
9	**Baltimore**	.417

(*Played only one season.) Since 1900, the only rival to the A.L. and N.L. has been the Federal League, formed in 1914. Nine teams (they are ranked here by their two-year Federal League winning percentages) played for two seasons before the league broke up and the players returned to their former teams.

THE TOP 10
First National Association Teams

	TEAM	YEAR
1	**Philadelphia Athletics**	1871
2	**Chicago White Stockings**	1871
3	**Boston Red Stockings**	1871
4	**Washington Olympics**	1871
5	**New York Mutuals**	1871
6	**Troy Haymakers**	1871
7	**Fort Wayne Kekiongas**	1871
8	**Cleveland Forest Citys**	1871
9	**Rockford Forest Citys**	1871

The National Association existed from 1871–75. Some historians date the beginning of the Major Leagues to this league. This list reflects the order of finish in the N.A.'s first season. Two teams were added in 1872; by 1875, there were 13.

THE TOP 10
Most Recent AAGBL Champions

	TEAM	YEAR
1	**Kalamazoo Lassies**	1954
2	**Grand Rapids Chicks**	1953
3	**South Bend Blue Sox**	1952
4	**South Bend Blue Sox**	1951
5	**Rockford Peaches**	1950
6	**Rockford Peaches**	1949
7	**Rockford Peaches**	1948
8	**Grand Rapids Chicks**	1947
9	**Racine Belles**	1946
10	**Rockford Peaches**	1945

During World War II, entrepreneur Philip Wrigley, owner of the Chicago Cubs, created the All-American Girls Professional Baseball League to entertain fans missing the male players off fighting the war. The league began by playing fast-pitch softball but evolved into real baseball. The league was formed in 1943 and disbanded in 1954.

THE TOP 10
Most Recent AAGBL Players of the Year

	PLAYER, TEAM	YEAR
1	**Joanne Weaver,** Fort Wayne	1954
2	**Jean Faut,** South Bend	1953
3	**Betty Foss**, Fort Wayne	1952
4	**Jean Faut,** South Bend	1951
5	**Alma Ziegler**, Grand Rapids	1950
6	**Doris Sams,** Muskegon	1949
7	**Audrey Wagner**, Kenosha	1948
8	**Doris Sams,** Muskegon	1947
9	**Sophie Kurys,** Racine	1946
10	**Connie Wisniewski**, Grd. Rapids	1945

THE PLAYERS LEAGUE

One of the most remarkable and versatile individuals in baseball history was also partly responsible for one of the early challenges to the dominance of the Major Leagues. John Montgomery Ward was a league-leading pitcher for Providence of the National League; he pitched the second-ever perfect game in 1880. He later became a star shortstop with the New York Giants and a top basestealer. After earning a law degree in 1885 while still playing, he became involved in baseball labor issues and helped form the first "union," the Brotherhood of Professional Base Ball Players. In 1890, after their demands went unmet, dozens of players left their teams to form the Players League. Eight teams were formed, with Ward joining Brooklyn. But the Players League disbanded after only one season and the players went back to their former teams. Ward was elected to the Hall of Fame in 1964.

SNAP SHOTS

QUIZ TIME

Help in a pinch: What player holds the Major League record for most career pinch hits?
Hint: He set the record in 2001. See page 36.

35

BUNTS & PINCHES

THE TOP 10

Most Career Pinch Hits

PLAYER (SEASONS PLAYED)	PINCH HITS
1 **Lenny Harris*** (1988–)	179
2 **Manny Mota** (1962–82)	150
3 **Smoky Burgess** (1949–67)	145
4 **Greg Gross** (1973–89)	143
5= **Dave Hansen*** (1990–)	123
= **Jose Morales** (1973–84)	123
= **John Vander Wal*** (1991–)	123
8= **Jerry Lynch** (1954–66)	116
9 **Red Lucas** (1923–38)	114
10 **Steve Braun** (1971–85)	113

Successful pinch hitting has become a specialized skill. Players take the place of teammates at the plate in an effort to jump-start a team's offense.

THE TOP 10

Best Career Pinch Hitting Avg.*

PLAYER (SEASONS PLAYED)	BATTING AVERAGE
1 **Alex Arias*** (1992–)	.322
2 **Tommy Davis** (1959–76)	.320
3 **Frenchy Bordagaray** (1934–45)	.312
4 **Frankie Baumholtz** (1947–57)	.307
5 **Willie McGee** (1982–99)	.307
6 **Sid Bream** (1983–94)	.306
7 **Mark Carreon** (1987–96)	.306
8 **Red Schoendienst** (1945–63)	.303
9 **Bob Fothergill** (1922–33)	.300
10 **Dave Philley** (1941–62)	.299

*minimum 150 at-bats

Ten Most Intentional Walks

(Player/IBB)

1 Barry Bonds*, 484 **2 Hank Aaron**, 293 **3 Willie McCovey**, 260 **4 George Brett**, 229 **5 Willie Stargell**, 227 **6 Eddie Murray**, 222 **7 Frank Robinson**, 9218 **8 Ken Griffey, Jr.***, 204 **9 Tony Gwynn**, 203 **10 Mike Schmidt**, 201

THE TOP 10

Most Pinch Hit Home Runs

	BATTER (SEASONS PLAYED)	HOME RUNS
1	Cliff Johnson (1972-86)	20
2	Jerry Lynch (1954-66)	18
3	John Vander Wal* (1991-)	17
4 =	Gates Brown (1963-75)	16
=	Smoky Burgess (1949-67)	16
=	Willie McCovey (1959-80)	16
7 =	George Crowe (1952-61)	14
=	Dave Hansen* (1990-)	14
9	Glenallen Hill (1989-00)	13
10 =	Joe Adcock (1950-66)	12
=	Bob Cerv (1951-62)	12
=	Jose Morales (1973-84)	12
=	Graig Nettles (1967-88)	12

THE TOP 10

Most Recent 20-Game Losers

	PITCHER, SEASON	LOSSES
1	Mike Maroth*, 2003	21
2	Brian Kingman, 1981	20
3	Phil Niekro, 1979	20
4	Jerry Koosman, 1977	20
=	Phil Niekro, 1977	20
6	Wilbur Wood, 1975	20
7 =	Randy Jones, 1974	22
=	Bill Bonham, 1974	22
=	Steve Rogers, 1974	22
=	Mickey Lolich, 1974	21
=	Clyde Wright, 1974	20

GREAT IN A PINCH

In 16 seasons with eight Major League teams, Lenny Harris was always ready off the bench. His skill as a pinch-hitter helped him set the all-time record in 2001.

THE TOP 10

Most Complete Game 1–0 Wins

	PITCHER	CG 1–0 WINS
1	Walter Johnson	38
2	Grover Cleveland Alexander	17
3	Bert Blyleven	15
4	Christy Mathewson	14
5 =	Eddie Plank	13
=	Ed Walsh	13
=	Doc White	13
=	Cy Young	13
=	Dean Chance	13
10 =	Stan Coveleski	12
=	Gaylord Perry	12
=	Steve Carlton	12

THE TOP 10

Recent Annual Leaders in Sacrifice Bunts

YEAR	PLAYER	SAC. BUNTS
2003	Ramon Santiago*	17
2002	Jack Wilson*	22
2001 =	Tom Glavine*	17
=	Ricky Gutierrez*	17
=	Jack Wilson*	17
2000 =	Alex Gonzalez*	16
=	Ricky Gutierrez*	16
1999 =	Shane Reynolds	17
=	Omar Vizquel*	17
1998	Neifi Perez*	22
1997	Edgar Renteria*	19
1996	Tom Goodwin*	21
1995	Bobby Jones	18
1994	Ken Hill	16

A sacrifice bunt is when a player makes out on a bunt in order to advance a baserunner.

THE TOP 10

Most Times Grounding into a Double Play, Single-Season

	PLAYER (YEAR)	GIDP
1	Jim Rice (1984)	36
2	Jim Rice (1985)	35
3 =	Ben Grieve* (2000)	32
=	Jackie Jensen (1954)	32
=	Cal Ripken, Jr. (1985)	32
6 =	Tony Armas (1983)	31
=	Jim Rice (1983)	31
=	Ivan Rodriguez* (1999)	31
=	Bobby Doerr (1949)	31
10 =	Billy Hitchcock (1950)	30
=	Ernie Lombardi (1938)	30
=	Dave Winfield (1983)	30
=	Carl Yastrzemski (1964)	30
=	Brad Ausmus* (2002)	30

It's not a stat that players brag about, but it's part of the game. However, notice that many of these players are big RBI men for their teams. Their leadership in this category is an offshoot of their often being at bat with men on base. It also is a result of their hitting the ball hard, and, in most cases, their less than stellar speed.

Ten Most Career Sacrifice Flys

(Player/SFs)

1 Eddie Murray, 128 **2** Cal Ripken, Jr., 127 **3** Robin Yount, 123 **4** Hank Aaron, 121 **5** George Brett, 120 **6** Rusty Staub, 119 **7** Andre Dawson, 118 **8** Don Baylor, 115 **9** Brooks Robinson, 114 **10** Ruben Sierra*, 111

A sacrifice fly is awarded to a batter when a runner advances and scores after a fly ball hit by the batter is caught. The batter receives an RBI in this case, but does not get an official at-bat.

---

* Active through 2003

QUIZ TIME
Many fathers and sons have played in the Major Leagues. Can you name the father-son pair of pitchers who has combined to win the most games? Answer on page 39.

ODDS & ENDS

LAST MAN
Edward "Dutch" Zwilling played four Major League seasons.

First 10 Players Alphabetically

PLAYER (SEASONS PLAYED)

1 **Hank Aaron** (1954–76)
2 **Tommie Aaron** (1962–71)
3 **Don Aase** (1977–90)
4 **Andy Abad*** (2001–)
5 **John Abadie** (1875)
6 **Ed Abbaticchio** (1897–1910)
7 **Bert Abbey** (1892–96)
8 **Charlie Abbey** (1893–97)
9 **Fred Abbott** (1903–05)
10 **Jim Abbott** (1989–99)

Last 10 Players Alphabetically

PLAYER (SEASONS PLAYED)

1 **Dutch Zwilling** (1910, 1914–16)
2 **George Zuverink** (1951–59)
3 **Paul Zuvella** (1982–91)
4 **Frank Zupo** (1957–61)
5 **Bob Zupcic** (1991–94)
6 **Julio Zuleta** (2000)
7 **Bill Zuber** (1936–47)
8 **Jon Zuber** (1996–98)
9 **Eddie Zosky** (1991–92, '95, '99–2000)
10 **Sam Zoldak** (1944–52)

Most Hits, Last Name Johnson

Player (Seasons Played)/Hits

❶ **Bob Johnson** (1933–45), 2,051 ❷ **Lance Johnson** (1987–00), 1,565
❸ **Deron Johnson** (1960–76), 1,447 ❹ **Alex Johnson** (1964–76), 1,331
❺ **Cliff Johnson** (1972–86), 1,016 ❻ **Roy Johnson** (1929–38), 1,292
❼ **Davey Johnson** (1965–78), 1,252 ❽ **Howard Johnson** (1982–95), 1,229
❾ **Billy Johnson** (1943–53), 882 ❿ **Lamar Johnson** (1974–82), 755

Most Home Runs by Brothers

	PLAYERS (HRs)	TOTAL HRS
1	**Hank** (755) and **Tommie** (13) **Aaron**	768
2	**Joe** (361), **Vince** (125), and **Dom** (87) **DiMaggio**	573
3	**Eddie** (504) and **Rich** (4) **Murray**	508
3	**Jose** (462) and **Ozzie** (0) **Canseco**	462
4	**Cal** (431) and **Billy** (20) **Ripken**	451
5=	**Ken** (282), **Clete** (162), and **Cloyd** (0) **Boyer**	444
=	**Lee** (354) and **Carlos** (90) **May**	444
7	**Graig** (390) and **Jim** (16) **Nettles**	406
8	**Richie** (351), **Hank** (6), and **Ron** (1) **Allen**	358
9	**Bob** (288) and **Roy** (58) **Johnson**	346

Most Pitching Wins by Brothers

	PITCHERS (WINS)	TOTAL WINS
1	**Phil** (318) and **Joe** (221) **Niekro**	539
2	**Gaylord** (314) and **Jim** (215) **Perry**	529
3	**John** (326), **Dad** (39), and **Walter** (18) **Clarkson**	383
4	**Christy** (373) and **Henry** (0) **Mathewson**	373
5	**Pud** (361) and **Lou** (0) **Galvin**	361
6	**Ramon** (135) and **Pedro*** (166) **Martinez**	301
7	**Stan** (215) and **Harry** (81) **Coveleski**	296
8	**Bob** (168) and **Ken** (114) **Forsch**	282
9	**Rick** (214) and **Paul** (16) **Reuschel**	230
10	**Jesse** (152) and **Virgil** (61) **Barnes**	213

DOUBLE QUIZ TIME
What "iron" superstar holds the record for most grand slam home runs in a career? What switch-hitter slugged the most home runs? See 40–41 for both answers.

THE TOP 10

Most Home Runs by Fathers and Sons

PLAYERS (HRS)	TOTAL HRs
1 **Bobby** (332) and **Barry*** (658) **Bonds**	990
2 **Ken, Sr.** (152) and **Ken Jr.*** (481) **Griffey**	633
3 **Felipe** (206) and **Moises*** (239) **Alou**	445
4 **Tony** (379) and **Eduardo*** (58) **Perez**	437
5 **Bob** (105) and **Bret*** (221) and **Aaron*** (92) **Boone**	418
6 **Gus** (206) and **Buddy** (201) **Bell**	407
7 **Yogi** (358) and **Dale** (9) **Berra**	367
8 **Sandy Sr.** (13) **Sandy, Jr.*** (109), **Roberto***(206) **Alomar**	328
9 **Hal** (191) and **Brian** (103) **McRae**	294
10 **Buddy** (201) and **David** (85) **Bell**	286

THE TOP 10

Most Pitching Wins by Fathers and Sons

FATHER/SON (CAREER WINS)	TOTAL WINS
1 **Mel, Sr.** (164) and **Todd*** (138) **Stottlemyre**	302
2 **Dizzy** (170) and **Steve** (88) **Trout**	258
3 **Jim** (127) and **Jim, Jr.** (97) **Bagby**	224
4 **Ed** (195) and **Ed, Jr.** (11) **Walsh**	206
5 **Joe** (52) and **Joe; Jr.** (142) **Coleman**	194
6 **Clyde** (100) and **Jaret*** (37) **Wright**	137
7 **Ross** (0) and **Ross, Jr.** (124) **Grimsley**	124
8 **Julio** (7) and **Jaime** (116) **Navarro**	123
9 **Joe** (117) and **Joe, Jr.** (0) **Wood**	117
10 **Dick** (115) and **Steve** (1) **Ellsworth**	116

THE TOP 10

Longest Surnames

ALL TIED WITH 13 LETTERS

1=	**Gene DeMontreville** (1894–1904)
=	**Lee DeMontreville** (1903)
=	**Kirk Dressendorfer** (1991)
=	**Todd Hollandsworth*** (1995–)
=	**Al Hollingsworth** (1935–46)
=	**Bonnie Hollingsworth** (1922–28)
=	**Austin Knickerbocker** (1947)
=	**Bill Knickerbocker** (1933–42)
=	**Lou Schiappacasse** (1902)
=	**Ossee Schreckengost** (1897–1908)
=	**Tim Spooneybarger*** (2001–)
=	**William Van Landingham** (1994–97)

With a seven-letter first name, Van Landingham (right), who pitched in this very crowded jersey for the Giants, earns the top spot for longest full name of all time in baseball.

LONG NAME, SHORT CAREER

Van Landingham was a starting pitcher who finished his four-year Major League career (1994–97) with a 27–26 record.

* Active through 2003

HOME RUNS

Most Home Runs by a Righthanded Batter

BATTER (SEASONS PLAYED)	HOME RUNS
1 Hank Aaron (1954–76)	755
2 Willie Mays (1951–73)	660
3 Frank Robinson (1956–76)	586
4 Mark McGwire (1986–2001)	583
5 Harmon Killebrew (1954–75)	573
6 Mike Schmidt (1972–89)	548
7 Sammy Sosa* (1989–)	539
8 Jimmie Foxx (1925–45)	534
9 Ernie Banks (1953–71)	512
10 Dave Winfield (1973–95)	465

Most Home Runs by a Lefthanded Batter

BATTER (SEASONS PLAYED)	HOME RUNS
1 Babe Ruth (1914–35)	714
2 Barry Bonds* (1986–)	658
3 Reggie Jackson (1967–87)	563
4 Rafael Palmeiro* (1986–)	528
5= Willie McCovey (1959–80)	521
= Ted Williams (1939–60)	521
7 Eddie Mathews (1952–68)	512
8 Mel Ott (1926–47)	511
9 Lou Gehrig (1923–39)	493
10 Fred McGriff* (1986–)	491

Most Consecutive Seasons with 20 or More Home Runs

PLAYER (CONSEC. SEASONS)	NO. OF SEASONS
1 Hank Aaron (1955–74)	20
2 Babe Ruth (1919–1934)	16
3 Willie Mays (1954–68)	15
4= Eddie Mathews (1952–65)	14
= Mike Schmidt (1974–87)	14
= Barry Bonds* (1990–2003)	14
7= Billy Williams (1961–73)	13
= Willie Stargell (1964–76)	13
= Reggie Jackson (1968–80)	13
= Rafael Palmeiro* (1986–)	13

Most Home Runs by Switch Hitter

Batter (Seasons Played) Home Runs

1 Mickey Mantle (1951–68) 536 2 Eddie Murray (1977–97) 504
3 Chili Davis (1981–99) 350 4 Reggie Smith (1966–82) 314
5 Bobby Bonilla (1986–2001) 287 6 Ruben Sierra* (1986–) 285
7 Chipper Jones* (1993–) 280 8 Ted Simmons (1968–88) 248
9 Ken Singleton (1970–84) 246 10 Mickey Tettleton (1984–97) 245

SURPRISE SLUGGER

Pitchers don't normally hit a lot of home runs. In fact, the single-season record is 9. Jim Tobin is the only pitcher to hit 3 home runs in one game; he did it in 1942. Colorado's Mike Hampton made a big stir in 2001 with a 7-homer season. Rarer than a homer-hitting hurler is a player who hits two grand slams in one game. On July 3, 1966, pitcher Tony Cloninger (left) of the Atlanta Braves bucked the odds by doing just that in a 17–3 win over San Francisco. He had also hit two homers in his previous game.

SNAP SHOTS

Most Seasons of 40 or More Home Runs

PLAYER	NO. OF SEASONS
1 Babe Ruth	11
2= Hank Aaron	8
= Harmon Killebrew	8
4= Ken Griffey, Jr.*	7
= Barry Bonds*	7
= Sammy Sosa*	7
7= Willie Mays	6
= Mark McGwire	6
= Alex Rodriguez*	6
10= Eight players tied with	5

Alex Rodriguez's 47 homers in 2003 gave him six straight 40-homer seasons, helping him earn his first A.L. MVP award.

* Active through 2003

Top 10 Most Recent Players Hitting Four Home Runs in a Game

	PLAYER, TEAM	DATE
1	**Carlos Delgado**, Toronto	September 25, 2003
2	**Shawn Green**, Los Angeles	May 23, 2002
3	**Mike Cameron**, Seattle	May 2, 2002
4	**Mark Whiten**, St. Louis	September 7, 1993
5	**Bob Horner**, Atlanta	July 6, 1986
6	**Mike Schmidt**, Philadelphia	April 17, 1976
7	**Willie Mays**, San Francisco	April 30, 1961
8	**Rocky Colavito**, Cleveland	June 10, 1959
9	**Joe Adcock**, Milwaukee	July 31, 1954
10	**Gil Hodges**, Brooklyn	August 31, 1950

IN THE CLUTCH

Among his 493 career homers, Lou Gehrig had a record 23 "grand salamis." Playing on a high-scoring team like the powerful Yankees of the 1920s and 1930s helped a little .

THE TOP 10

Most Career Grand Slams

	PLAYER	GRAND SLAMS
1	**Lou Gehrig**	23
2	**Eddie Murray**	19
3	**Willie McCovey**	18
4=	**Jimmie Foxx**	17
=	**Ted Williams**	17
6=	**Hank Aaron**	16
=	**Dave Kingman**	16
=	**Babe Ruth**	16
=	**Robin Ventura***	16
10	**Manny Ramirez***	15

WORD PLAY

Among the dozens of nicknames or phrases for home runs: dinger, tater, goin' yard, gonzo, four-bagger, circuit clout, big fly, round-tripper, parkin' it, long ball, jack, belt.

MORE ODDS & ENDS

Best Team Nicknames

	NICKNAME (ERA, IF APPLICABLE)	TEAM
1	**Big Red Machine** (1970s)	Cincinnati Reds
2	**Bronx Bombers**	New York Yankees
3	**Old Towne Team**	Boston Red Sox
4	**The Friars**	San Diego Padres
5	**The Cardiac Kids** (1950s)	Philadephia Phillies
6	**The Gashouse Gang** (1930s)	St. Louis Cardinals
7	**The Halos**	Anaheim Angels
8	**The Tribe**	Cleveland Indians
9	**Pale Hose**	Chicago White Sox
10	**The Lords of Flatbush** (1950s)	Brooklyn Dodgers

This is a completely subjective list, and we hope that you can think of lots of other team nicknames that deserve a mention. The list combines nicknames that were used for teams during specific eras, as well as nicknames in everyday use. Many of the nicknames were first coined by writers looking for another way to refer to the teams they covered.

A REAL VETERAN PITCHER
Satchel Paige came out of retirement in 1965 to throw one game for the Kansas City Athletics at the "tender" age of 59.

Best Nicknames, Retired Players

	PLAYER	NICKNAME
1	**Jack Chapman**	Death to Flying Things
2	**Babe Ruth***	Sultan of Swat
3	**Reggie Jackson**	Mr. October
4	**Ted Williams**	The Splendid Splinter
5	**Joe DiMaggio**	The Yankee Clipper
6	**Willie Mays**	Say Hey Kid
7	**Dick Stuart**	Dr. Strangeglove
8	**Bill Lee**	Spaceman
9	**Stan Musial**	The Man
10	**Harold Reese**	Pee Wee

This is a completely subjective list. Please feel free to make your own. There have been hundreds of great nicknames in baseball history. We chose these as the most unique and memorable. Why was Chapman called that? He was a great fielder, and made a lot of great catches. The "flying things" were baseballs! (*Babe was a nickname for George Herman Ruth.)

The Ten Most Most-Retired Numbers

(Uniform Number/Teams)

❶ **42**, 30 ❷ **4**, 8 ❸ = **1**,7; = **20**,7
❺ **3**, 6; = **5**, 6 ❼ = **8**, 5; = **9**, 5;
= **14**, 5; = **34**, 5 ❿ = **6**, 4; = **19**, 4;
= **32**, 4; = **44**, 4

To honor their greatest players, teams "retire" uniform numbers, meaning that no player on that team will ever wear that number again. The numbers are displayed at the ballpark, often as large signs on the outfield wall or on the bleachers. The first number retired was Lou Gehrig's number 4 in 1939 by the Yankees. In 1997, to honor Jackie Robinson on the fiftieth anniversary of his rookie season, Robinson's number 42 was officially retired by Major League Baseball.

Oldest Player, Each Position

	POSITION	PLAYER (SEASON)	AGE
1	Manager	**Connie Mack**	87
2	Pitcher	**Satchel Paige** (1965)	59
3	DH	**Minnie Miñoso** (1976)	53
4	Outfielder	**Nick Altrock** (1929)	53
5	Catcher	**Jim O'Rourke** (1904)	52
6	=3rd Base	**Jimmy Austin** (1929)	49
	=2nd Base	**Arlie Latham** (1909)	49
8	=1st Base	**Dan Brouthers** (1904)	46
	=1st Base	**Cap Anson** (1897)	46
10	Shortstop	**Bobby Wallace** (1918)	44

Manager is not a position, true, but otherwise our list would have been less than a "top ten."

DID YOU KNOW?
The highest retired uniform number is Carlton Fisk's number 72 by the White Sox. Fisk created that number by reversing the numerals of his old number with the Red Sox.

TEAMS

O CANADA!

Joe Carter and the Toronto Blue Jays celebrate the 1992 World Series championship, the first ever won by a team from outside the United States. They would repeat the feat the next season.

Expansion Teams with the Best First–Season Records

TEAM (YEAR)	WIN PCT. (RECORD)
1 **Angels** (1961)	.438 (70–90)
2 **Royals** (1969)	.426 (69–93)
3 **Rockies** (1993)	.414 (67–95)
4 **Diamondbacks** (1998)	.401 (65–97)
5 **Colt .45s** (1962)	.400 (64–96)
6= **Pilots** (1969)	.395 (64–98)
= **Mariners** (1977)	.395 (64–98)
= **Marlins** (1993)	.395 (64–98)
9 **Devil Rays** (1998)	.389 (63–99)
10 **Blue Jays** (1977)	.335 (54–107)

Expansion teams are formed by an expansion draft of players from other teams, as well as minor league players and college and high school draft picks. It usually takes a team several seasons to improve, but the Arizona Diamondbacks won the World Series in their fourth season.

Most Victories by a Team, All–Time

TEAM	VICTORIES
1 **N.Y./S.F. Giants**	9,871
2 **Chicago Cubs**	9,667
3 **Brooklyn/L.A. Dodgers**	9,542
4 **St. Louis Cardinals**	9,478
5 **Cincinnati Reds**	9,371
6 **Pittsburgh Pirates**	9,350
7 **Bos./Mil./Atl. Braves**	9,347
8 **New York Yankees**	8,996
9 **Philadelphia Phillies**	8,505
10 **Boston Red Sox**	8,165

The Ten Newest MLB Teams
Team/Year Founded

1 = **Arizona Diamondbacks**, 1998; = **Tampa Bay Devil Rays**, 1998 **3** = **Colorado Rockies**, 1993; = **Florida Marlins**, 1993 **5** = **Seattle Mariners**, 1977; = **Toronto Blue Jays**, 1977; **7** = **San Diego Padres**, 1969; = **Montreal Expos**, 1969; = **Milwaukee Brewer**s, 1969 **10** **Kansas City Royals**, 1968

Major League Baseball welcomes new teams through the "expansion" process. Ownership groups must meet hundreds of criteria before a new franchise is created. Note: The Brewers played one season as the Seattle Pilots before moving to Milwaukee.

WINNING HIT

Florida shortstop Edgar Renteria hits the game-winning single in the bottom of the 11th inning in Game 7 of the 1997 World Series, making the young Marlins the champs.

DID YOU KNOW?
The Montreal Expos were named for Expo 67, a World's Fair-like event held in Montreal two years before the team was founded.

Oldest Teams in the American League

TEAM	YEAR FOUNDED
1 = **Boston Red Sox**	1901
= **Chicago White Sox**	1901
= **Cleveland Indians**	1901
= **Detroit Tigers**	1901
= **Oakland Athletics**	1901
= **Baltimore Orioles**	1901
= **Minnesota Twins**	1901
= **New York Yankees**	1901
9 = **Texas Rangers**	1961
= **Anaheim Angels**	1961

The American League was formed in 1901. Four franchises survive in their hometowns: Boston, Chicago, Cleveland, and Detroit. Among other original A.L. teams, the Orioles played one season (1901) in Milwaukee before moving to St. Louis as the Browns; the Twins began play as the Washington Senators, then moved to Minnesota in 1961. The Athletics first played in Philadelphia, later moving to Kansas City and then to Oakland. Since it was created after the National League, the A.L. is still sometimes referred to as the "junior circuit."

Oldest Teams in the National League

TEAM	YEAR FOUNDED
1 = **Chicago Cubs**	1876
= **Atlanta Braves**	1876
3 = **Cincinnati Reds**	1882
= **St. Louis Cardinals**	1882
= **Pittsburgh Pirates**	1882
6 = **San Francisco Giant**s	1883
= **Philadelphia Phillies**	1883
8 **Los Angeles Dodgers**	1884
9 = **New York Mets**	1962
= **Houston Astros**	1962
10 = **Montreal Expos**	1969
= **San Diego Padres**	1969

The National League was formed in 1876, and was made up of some new teams and some teams from the National Association, another pro league. The dates of "founding" for the first two teams listed note their entry in the new N.L.; both of these clubs had existed in some form or another prior to that date. Also, while the Cincinnati Red Stockings were the first pro team to form in 1869, that club had no relation to the Cincinnati Reds of today.

Oldest Defunct "Major" League Franchises

TEAM	YEAR DISBANDED
1 = **Forest City of Rockford, Ill.**	1871
= **Kekionga of Fort Wayne**	1871
= **White Stockings of Chicago**	1871
4 = **Forest City of Cleveland**	1872
= **Olympic of Washington D.C.**	1872
= **Haymakers of Troy, N.Y.**	1872
= **Eckford of Brooklyn**	1872
= **Mansfield of Middletown, Ct.**	1872
9 = **Maryland of Baltimore**	1873
= **National of Washington D.C.**	1873
= **Resolute of Elizabeth, N.J.**	1873

These are some of the clubs that lasted only a short time in the original National Association, which played from 1871–75 and predated the National League. In those days, teams were formed by athletic clubs, i.e., the Eckford Athletic Club of Brooklyn. In baseball's early days, teams sometimes disbanded in the middle of a season or "morphed" into other franchises with the exchange of little more than a handshake between the owners or organizers. Note the small cities that had pro teams in those days, compared to the major metropolises that play host to teams today.

O CANADA!

While baseball has long been played in the Great White North, Canada did not have a Major League franchise until 1969, when the Montreal Expos joined the National League. In 1992, the Toronto Blue Jays, who played their first season in the American League in 1977, became the first team outside the United States to win the World Series, which they also won in 1993. The Expos have been less successful, reaching the NLCS in 1981. Canada also is home to minor league teams in Edmonton, Calgary, Ottawa, Vancouver, and Medicine Hat, among others.

SNAP SHOTS

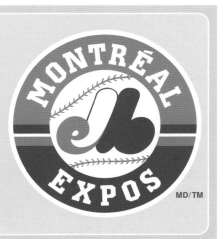

Bill Dickey, Lou Gehrig, Joe DiMaggio, and Tony Lazzeri are just four of the stars that have helped the Yankees set the record for winning percentage.

Most Victories by a Team, Single Season

Team (Year)/Victories

❶ **Chicago Cubs** (1906), 116
= **Seattle Mariners** (2001), 116
❸ **New York Yankees** (1998), 114
❹ **Cleveland Indians** (1954), 111
❺ = **Pittsburgh Pirates** (1909), 110;
= **New York Yankees** (1927), 110
❼ **New York Yankees** (1961), 109;
= **Baltimore Orioles** (1969), 109
❾ **Baltimore Orioles** (1970), 108
❿ **New York Mets** (1986), 108

Victories in the postseason are not included. With the addition of an extra round of playoffs (the Division Series), the Yankees' total of 125 victories in 1998 is the most by any team when the regular season, playoffs, and World Series are combined.

THE TOP 10
Most Losses by a Team, Single Season*

	TEAM (YEAR)	LOSSES
1	New York Mets (1962)	120
2	Philadelphia Athletics (1917)	117
3	Boston Braves (1935)	115
4	Washington Senators (1904)	113
5 =	Pittsburgh Pirates (1952)	112
=	New York Mets (1965)	112
7 =	New York Mets (1963)	111
=	Philadelphia Phillies (1941)	111
=	St. Louis Browns (1939)	111
=	Boston Red Sox (1932)	111

THE TOP 10
Most Runs Scored by a Team, Single Season*

	TEAM (YEAR)	RUNS
1	New York Yankees (1931)	1,067
2	New York Yankees (1936)	1,065
3	New York Yankees (1930)	1,062
4	Boston Red Sox (1950)	1,027
5	Cleveland Indians (1999)	1,009
6	St. Louis Cardinals (1930)	1,004
7	New York Yankees (1932)	1,002
8	Chicago Cubs (1930)	998
9	Seattle Mariners (1996)	993
10	Chicago Cubs (1929)	982

THE TOP 10
Most Strikeouts by a Team, Single Season*

	TEAM, YEAR	STRIKEOUTS
1	Chicago Cubs, 2001	1,344
2 =	Arizona Diamondbacks, 2001	1,297
=	New York Yankees, 2001	1,266
4	Boston Red Sox, 2001	1,259
5	Atlanta Braves, 1996	1,245
6 =	Los Angeles Dodgers, 1997	1,232
=	Atlanta Braves, 1998	1,232
8	Houston Astros, 2001	1,228
9	Cleveland Indians, 2001	1,218
10	New York Mets, 1990	1,217
10	San Diego Padres, 1998	1,217

QUIZ TIME?
What slugger hit the most home runs hit by a third baseman? (Answer on page 48.)

THE TOP 10

Total Games Played

TEAM (YEAR)	GAMES
1 **Chicago Cubs**	18,473
2 **Atlanta Braves**	18,443
3 **Cincinnati Reds**	18,076
4 **St. Louis Cardinals**	18,069
5 **Pittsburgh Pirates**	18,039
6 **San Francisco Giants**	17,939
7 **Philadelphia Phillies**	17,911
8 **Los Angeles Dodgers**	17,876
9 **Detroit Tigers**	15,624
10 **Minnesota Twins**	15,589

Not surprisingly, these are the oldest teams in the Major Leagues...or should we say oldest franchises? While teams may move to new homes, the MLB franchise and its records remain intact. The Braves began play in Boston and moved first to Milwaukee before settling in Atlanta in 1966. The Giants and Dodgers both played in New York until 1958. Oh, yes...the Twins? Didn't they just start playing in 1961? Yes, they did, as the Twins, but the franchise dates back to 1901, when they began play as the Washington Senators.

Top Ten Best All-Time Records, by Percentage

Team/All-Time Pct.

❶ **Yankees**, .565 ❷ **Giants**, .539
❸ **Dodgers**, .524 ❹ **Cubs**, .515
❺ **Cardinals**, .514 ❻ = **Red Sox**, .512;
= **Indians**, .512; = **Tigers** .511
❾ = **Reds** .510; = **Pirates** .510

Winning percentage is calculated by dividing the number of wins by the number of total games. For instance, a record of 6 wins and 4 losses gives a percentage of .600 (6/10). This top 10 doesn't include recent expansion teams, otherwise the Arizona Diamondbacks, born in 1998, would be listed third all-time.

THE TOP 10

Most Shutouts Pitched by a Team, Single Season

TEAM (YEAR)	SHUTOUTS
1= **Chicago White Sox** (1906)	32
= **Chicago Cubs** (1907)	32
= **Chicago Cubs** (1909)	32
4= **Chicago Cubs** (1906)	30
= **St. Louis Cardinals** (1968)	30
6 **Chicago Cubs** (1908)	29
7= **Los Angeles Angels** (1964)	28
= **New York Mets** (1969)	28
9= **Cleveland Indians** (1906)	27
= **Pittsburgh Pirates** (1906)	27
= **Philadelphia Athletics** (1907)	27
= **Philadelphia Athletics** (1909)	27

Good pitching helps. The White Sox won the World Series in '06, while the Cubs won in '07 and '08.

THE MEN IN CHARGE

Manager Joe Torre (right) led the Yankees to a quartet of World Series titles; his first was in 1996 and he won three from 1992–2000. Torre is the latest in a long line of great Yankees managers. Casey Stengel led the great Yankee teams of the 1940s and 1950s (he later led the Mets to a record 120 losses in 1962). "The Old Perfesser" won seven Series, including five in a row from 1949–53. Joe McCarthy also won seven championships, including four straight from 1936–39. Miller Huggins was the Yankee skipper from 1918–1929 and won three championships. While the Yankees' players have been the main reason for their success, they have been blessed with a succession of Hall of Fame managers who molded that great talent and kept the New York Yankees winning.

SNAP SHOTS

THE TOP 10

Most Home Runs by a Team, Single Season

TEAM (YEAR)	HOME RUNS
1 **Seattle Mariners** (1997)	267
2 **Baltimore Orioles** (1996)	257
3 **Houston Astros** (2000)	249
4 **Texas Rangers** (2001)	246
5 **Seattle Mariners** (1996)	245
6= **Seattle Mariners** (1999)	244
= **Toronto Blue Jays** (2000)	244
8 **Oakland Athletics** (1996)	243
9 **New York Yankees** (1961)	240
10= **Colorado Rockies** (1996)	239
= **Colorado Rockies** (2000)	239

Proving that a bunch of home runs does not a champion make, only one of these top ten single-season home run record-holders went on to win the World Series in the same year that they made this list. The Yankees defeated the Reds in 1961, outhomering Cincinnati 7 to 3 to help them take the title in five games.

* Since 1900

GRABBING FIRST PLACE

Speedy outfielder Kenny Lofton helped the Indians dominate the American League Central Division in 1995. The Tribe finished 30 games ahead of second-place Kansas City. Unfortunately, Cleveland lost in the World Series to Atlanta.

THE TOP 10
Largest Winning Margin in a Season

	TEAM (YEAR)	# OF GAMES AHEAD OF SECOND-PLACE TEAM
1	Cleveland Indians (1995)	30.0
2	Pittsburgh Pirates (1902)	27.5
3	New York Yankees (1998)	22.0
4=	New York Mets (1986)	21.5
=	Cleveland Indians (1999)	21.5
6	Atlanta Braves (1995)	21.0
7=	Chicago Cubs (1906)	20.0
=	Cincinnati Reds (1975)	20.0
=	Chicago White Sox (1983)	20.0
10	New York Yankees (1936)	19.5

The Major Leagues divided into four divisions in 1969, so margins that year and after are for division championships. Before 1969, the margins reflect league championships. Teams can finish "half-games" ahead of or behind one another in the standings. To determine the margin in "games," add the differences between two teams' wins and losses, respectively, then divide by two.

THE TOP 10
Longest Losing Streak by a Team

	TEAM (YEAR)	CONSECUTIVE LOSSES
1	Philadelphia Phillies (1961)	23
2	Baltimore Orioles (1988)	21
3=	Boston Red Sox (1906)	20
=	Philadelphia Athletics (1916)	20
=	Philadelphia Athletics (1943)	20
=	Montreal Expos (1969)	20
7	Boston Braves (1906)	19
=	Cincinnati Reds (1914)	19
=	Detroit Tigers (1975)	19
10=	Philadelphia Athletics (1920)	18
=	Washington Senators (1948)	18
=	Washington Senators (1959)	18

THE TOP 10
Longest Winning Streak by a Team

	TEAM (YEAR)	CONSECUTIVE VICTORIES
1	New York Giants (1916)	26
2	Chicago Cubs (1935)	21
3	Oakland Athletics (2002)	20
4=	Chicago White Sox (1906)	19
=	New York Yankees (1947)	19
6=	New York Giants (1904)	18
=	New York Yankees (1953)	18
8=	New York Giants (1907)	17
=	New York Giants (1916)	17
=	Washington Senators (1912)	17
=	Philadelphia Athletics (1931)	17

The Giants streak in 1916 wasn't enough to win the league. They finished fourth.

THE TOP 10
Lowest Team ERA in a Season*

	TEAM (YEAR)	ERA
1	Chicago Cubs (1907)	1.73
2=	Chicago Cubs (1909)	1.75
=	Chicago Cubs (1906)	1.75
4	Philadelphia Athletics (1910)	1.79
5	Philadelphia Athletics (1909)	1.93
6	Chicago White Sox (1905)	1.99
7	Cleveland Indians (1908)	2.02
8	Chicago White Sox (1910)	2.03
9	Chicago Cubs (1905)	2.04
10	Chicago White Sox (1909)	2.05

QUIZ TIME

The hottest stat in baseball is OPS: on-base percentage plus slugging percentage. Can you name the expansion team that has posted the best all-time team OPS? See page 51.

HOT CORNER HOMERS

Philadelphia's Mike Schmidt is perhaps the best all-around third baseman in baseball history. For sure, he has hit more homers than any other man who has played the "hot corner." Schmidt was elected to the Hall of Fame in 1995.

THE TOP 10

Highest Team Batting Average in a Season*

	TEAM (YEAR)	BATTING AVERAGE
1	**New York Giants** (1930)	.319
2	**Detroit Tigers** (1921)	.316
3	**Philadelphia Phillies** (1930)	.315
4	**St. Louis Cardinals** (1930)	.314
5	**St. Louis Browns** (1922)	.313
6=	**New York Yankees** (1930)	.309
=	**Pittsburgh Pirates** (1928)	.309
=	**Philadelphia Phillies** (1929)	.309
=	**Chicago Cubs** (1930)	.309
10	**St. Louis Browns** (1920)	.308

* Since 1900

Leading the league in team batting average (calculated by dividing total team hits into total team at-bats) doesn't guarantee success. Of the teams on this top 10 list, only the 1930 Cardinals made it to the World Series (and they lost that to the Athletics). Four N.L. teams from 1930 are on this list. No surprise there: The average for the entire league was .304, the only time a single league has topped .300.

THE TOP 10

Individual Team Leaders in Wins

	PLAYER, TEAM	WINS
1	**Walter Johnson**, Senators	417
2	**Christy Mathewson**, Giants	372
3	**Warren Spahn**, Braves	356
4	**Eddie Plank**, Athletics	284
5	**Jim Palmer**, Orioles	268
6	**Bob Feller**, Indians	266
7	**Ted Lyons**, White Sox	260
8	**Bob Gibson**, Cardinals	251
9	**Steve Carlton**, Phillies	241
10	**Don Sutton**, Dodgers	233

This list ranks the top 10 players who are one team's all-time leader in pitching victories. Notice, for instance, that Warren Spahn's total here of 356 wins, most in Braves history, differs from his all-time total of 363, since he also earned wins later in his career with the Mets and Giants. And Ted Lyons's 260 victories for the White Sox are well down the all-time list for all players, but were enough to make him the Pale Hose's all-time leader. Steve Carlton is another 300-game winner, but he also won games for five other teams.

THE TOP 10

Individual Team Leaders in Home Runs

	PLAYER, TEAM	HOME RUNS
1	**Hank Aaron**, Braves	733
2	**Babe Ruth**, Yankees	659
3	**Willie Mays**, Giants	646
4	**Harmon Killebrew**, Twins	559
5	**Ted Williams**, Red Sox	521
6	**Ernie Banks,** Cubs	512
7	**Mike Schmidt**, Phillies	548
8=	**Willie Stargell**, Pirates	475
=	**Stan Musial**, Cardinals	475
10	**Cal Ripken, Jr.**, Orioles	431

This list ranks the top 10 players who hold single-team career records for home runs. Willie Mays's Giants record of 646 homers differs from his all-time career total of 660, since he hit 14 home runs for the New York Mets at the end of his career. Also, although Frank Robinson may be fifth all-time with 586 home runs, he split his career with several teams.

TEAM RECORDS

Most Home Runs by a Team, All-Time

	TEAM	TOTAL HOME RUNS
1	N.Y. Yankees	12,798
2	N.Y./S.F. Giants	12,540
3	Chicago Cubs	11,509
4	Bos./Mil./Atl. Braves	11,339
5	Detroit Tigers	11,062
6	Boston Red Sox	10,678
7	Phil./K.C./Oak. Athletics	10,574
8	Cincinnati Reds	10,472
9	Baltimore Orioles	10,458
10	Philadelphia Phillies	10,413

Most Stolen Bases by a Team, All-Time

	TEAM	STOLEN BASES
1	Cincinnati Reds	16,009
2	St. Louis Cardinals	15,729
3	Brooklyn/L.A. Dodgers	15,332
4	N.Y./S.F. Giants	14,965
5	Chicago Cubs	14,055
6	Pittsburgh Pirates	13,941
7	Philadelphia Phillies	12,807
8	Bos./Mil./Atl. Braves	12,488
9	Chicago White Sox	11,779
10	Phil./K.C./Oak. Athletics	10,409

Most Stolen Bases by a Team in a Season*

	TEAM	STOLEN BASES
1	New York Giants (1911)	347
2	Oakland Athletics (1976)	341
3	New York Giants (1912)	319
4	St. Louis Cardinals (1985)	314
5	Cincinnat Reds (1910)	310
6	New York Giants (1913)	296
7	New York Giants (1905)	291
8	Cincinnati Reds (1906)	289
9=	New York Giants (1906)	288
=	New York Yankees (1910)	288

Since 1900

SLIDE, MAURY, SLIDE

Shortstop Maury Wills is safe at second with his 104th stolen base of 1962, setting a single-season record (later broken by several players) and adding to the Los Angeles Dodgers' all-time stolen-base total.

THE TOP 10

Most Days in First Place

TEAM, YEAR (POSSIBLE DAYS)*	DAYS
1 Baltimore Orioles, 1997 (182)	182
2 =Detroit Tigers#, 1984 (182)	181
=Philadelphia Phillies, 1993 (182)	181
=Cleveland Indians, 1998 (181)	181
5 =Cleveland Indians, 1999 (182)	179
=St. Louis Cardinals, 2000 (182)	179
7 =Cincinnati Reds, 1970 (179)	178
=Cincinnati Reds#, 1990 (178)	178
9 =L.A. Dodgers, 1974 (181)	177
=Oakland Athletics, 1988 (182)	177
=Texas Rangers, 1996 (183)	177

* Number of possible days per season in parentheses

It is a rare feat indeed for a team to win "wire to wire," that is, lead its division or league every single day of a season. But domination in the regular season doesn't always pay off with a World Series title. Of these ten teams who romped through the summer, only two (#) ended up as the overall champion.

CANADIAN ROCKIE
Colorado Rockies outfielder Larry Walker grew up playing hockey in Canada but has become one of baseball's best all-around hitters.

THE TOP 10

Most RBI by a Team, All-Time

TEAM	RBI
1 Chicago Cubs	78,070
2 N.Y./S.F. Giants	77,434
3 Bos./Mil./Atl. Braves	77,048
4 St. Louis Cardinals	74,994
5 Cincinnati Reds	74,458
6 Pittsburgh Pirates	73,493
7 Philadelphia Phillies	73,324
8 Brooklyn/L.A. Dodgers	73,147
9 New York Yankees	71,092
10 Boston Red Sox	67,643

THE TOP 10

Most Strikeouts by a Team's Pitchers, All-Time

TEAM	STRIKEOUTS
1 Brooklyn/L.A. Dodgers	85,588
2 Chicago Cubs	83,605
3 N.Y./S.F. Giants	82,277
4 Philadelphia Phillies	78,860
5 St. Louis Cardinals	78,686
6 Bos./Mil./Atl. Braves	78,355
7 Cincinnati Reds	77,024
8 Pittsburgh Pirates	75,616
9 New York Yankees	73,719
10 Cleveland Indians	73,232

THE TOP 10

Highest Team OPS, All-Time

TEAM	ALL-TIME OPS
1 Colorado Rockies	804
2 Arizona Diamondbacks	762
3 Seattle Mariners	744
4 Toronto Blue Jays	742
5 New York Yankees	736
6 Florida Marlins	726
7 Boston Red Sox	724
8 Kansas City Royals	722
9 Detroit Tigers	721
10 =Milwaukee Brewers	720
=Tampa Bay Devil Rays	720

The more powerful overall offenses of today's game give newer clubs an advantage in these all-time, cumulative categories. Of the teams on this list, only three (New York, Boston, and Detroit) played before 1969. For an explanation of OPS, see page 13.

It's probably not the record they're most proud of, but the Chicago Cubs hold the all-time record for most errors by a team with 27,539.

TRIPLE THREAT

"Wahoo" Sam Crawford, whose hometown of Wahoo, Nebraska, gave him his nickname, is the all-time leader with 309 triples.

THE TOP 10

Most All-Time Triples, Team

	TEAM	TRIPLES
1	Pittsburgh Pirates	7,885
2	Chicago Cubs	6,694
3	St. Louis Cardinals	6,509
4	Cincinnati Reds	6,341
5	Philadelphia Phillies	5,947
6	Detroit Tigers	5,448
7	Chicago White Sox	5,052
8	New York Yankees	5,043
9	Boston Red Sox	5,015
10	Cleveland Indians	4,933

Triples are becoming more and more rare in baseball, so this list doesn't figure to change too dramatically. For many years, the Pirates benefited from the huge outfield of their enormous old ballpark, Forbes Field.

THE TOP 10

Fewest Home Runs by a Team, Single-Season*

	TEAM, YEAR	HOME RUNS
1=	Chicago White Sox, 1908	4
=	Washington Senators, 1916	4
=	Washington Senators, 1917	4
4=	Philadelphia Phillies, 1902	5
=	Chicago White Sox, 1907	5
=	St. Louis Browns, 1918	5
7=	Chicago Cubs, 1902	6
=	New York Giants, 1902	6
9=	Chicago White Sox, 1906	7
=	Chicago White Sox, 1910	7

(*Since 1901.*) In the years before the advent of two Major Leagues (A.L. and N.L.), several teams fell below these home run totals. In fact, the 1875 White Stockings and 1877 Cubs both completed their seasons without hitting a single home run!

THE TOP 10

Highest All-Time Fielding Percentage, Team

	TEAM	PCT.
1	Arizona Diamondbacks	.984
2=	Colorado Rockies	.981
=	Toronto Blue Jays	.981
4=	Florida Marlins	.980
=	Tampa Bay Devil Rays	.980
=	Seattle Mariners	.980
7=	Kansas City Royals	.979
=	Milwaukee Brewers	.979
9=	Houston Astros	.978
=	Montreal Expos	.978
=	New York Mets	.978
=	Texas Rangers	.978

This list is dominated by expansion teams, for the simple reason that errors are far less common today than they once were. Fielding percentage is figured by subtracting errors from fielding chances and dividing the result by fielding chances.

Total Numbers of Minor League Teams by Year

(Year/Total)

① **2000**, 246 ② **1999**, 241 ③ **1998**, 242 ④ **1997**, 236 ⑤ **1996**, 218 ⑥ **1995**, 216 ⑦ **1994**, 216 ⑧ **1993**, 214 ⑨ **1992**, 212 ⑩ **1991**, 207

The number of minor league teams has risen steadily since the late 1970s. New stadiums, new team logos, and new marketing techniques have made minor-league baseball profitable for small cities and towns around the country. The heyday of the minors came in the late 1940s, when more than 400 teams crowded the summer calendar.

DID YOU KNOW?

Branch Rickey of the St. Louis Cardinals (and later the Dodgers) is credited with making minor-league "farm systems" part of every Major League team.

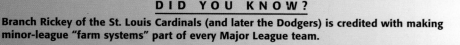

WE WON! WE WON!
The New York Mets celebrate their victory in a 1999 playoff game that gave them the wild-card spot in the N.L. Division Series.

Teams with Most Hall-of-Fame Players

TEAM	PLAYERS
1 N.Y./S.F. Giants	52
2=Bklyn./L.A. Dodgers	43
=Bos./Mil./Atl. Braves	43
4 St. Louis Cardinals	36
5=Chicago Cubs	35
=Cincinnati Reds	35
7 Pittsburgh Pirates	34
8 New York Yankees	33
9 Philadelphia Phillies	31
10 Boston Red Sox	28

This list shows which teams have had the most members of the Hall of Fame play for their club at any time, including brief appearances at the end or beginning of a career. There are only 253 people associated with a team who are members of the Hall, so obviously there is a lot of overlap—many players having been on several teams during their career.

Tiebreaking Playoff Games or Series

	SCORE	TIE BROKEN	DATE
1	Mets 5, Reds 0	N.L. wild card	10/4/99
2	Cubs 5, Giants 3	N.L. wild card	9/28/98
3	Mariners 9, Angels 1	A.L. West	10/2/95
4	Astros 7, Dodgers 1	N.L. West	10/6/80
5	Yankees 5, Red Sox 4	A.L. East	10/2/78
6	Giants 2, Dodgers 1#	N.L.	10/62
7	Dodgers 2, Braves 0#	N.L.	9/59
8	Giants 2, Dodgers 1#	N.L.	10/51
9	Indians 8, Red Sox 3	A.L.	10/4/48
10	Cardinals 2, Dodgers 0#	N.L.	10/46

Few things are more exciting in baseball than a final playoff game. The winning team carries on to play another day; the losing team goes home. Having two teams finish the season tied for a playoff spot is rare in baseball. When that happens, the two teams meet in a special playoff game or series. The results can be dramatic; the 1951 playoff between the Giants and Dodgers ended with Bobby Thomson's dramatic ninth-inning, three-run homer. For winners of these playoffs, the games are remembered among a team's finest moments. For the losers, they are a dark day in franchise history. (# Denotes three-game playoff series. Score is result in games.)

Most MVP Awards, Team

TEAM	TOTAL MVP AWARDS
1 Yankees	18
2 Cardinals	13
3 Reds	11
4=Red Sox	10
=Dodgers	10
=Giants	10
7 Athletics	9
8=Tigers	8
=Cubs	8
10=Phillies	6
= Pirates	6

The first Most Valuable Player awards were presented in 1931.

Top Ten Teams with the Most World Series Championships

	TEAM	W.S. TITLES
1	New York Yankees	26
2 =	St. Louis Cardinals	9
=	Oakland/Philadelphia Athletics	9
4	Los Angeles/Brooklyn Dodgers	6
5 =	San Francisco/New York Giants	5
=	Pittsburgh Pirates	5
=	Boston Red Sox	5
8	Detroit Tigers	4
9 =	Atlanta/Milwaukee/Boston Braves	3
=	Baltimore Orioles	3
=	Minnesota Twins/Washington Senators	3

The Yankees' total just jumps out at you—nearly three times as many as the Cardinals and Athletics. The Yankees have had mini-dynasties in the 1920s, the 1930s, the 1950s, the 1960s, and the 1990s.

BASEBALL NUT

The Phillie Phanatic does stunts on a 4-wheel ATV.

The Ten Coolest Mascots

Mascot/Team

❶ **Phillie Phanatic**, Phillies
❷ **Billy Marlin**, Marlins
❸ **Stomper the Elephant**, Athletics
❹ **The Bird**, Orioles ❺ **FredBird**, Cardinals ❻ **Pirate Parrot**, Pirates
❼ **Slugger**, Royals ❽ **Mr. Met**, Mets
❾ **Digger**, Rockies ❿ **Youppi**, Expos

This is admittedly a subjective ranking, so feel free to move them around to suit your own personal tastes. We would have included The Famous Chicken, who got his start with the San Diego Padres, but he's a freelance fowl now, not affiliated with any one team. Mascot Trivia: Billy Marlin once lost his head in a swamp. He was parachuting into the stadium before a game when his head fell off.

Most A.L. Championships

	TEAM	PENNANTS
1	New York Yankees	39
2	Athletics	15
3	Red Sox	10
4	Tigers	9
5	Orioles/Browns	7
6	Twins/Senators	6
7 =	White Sox	5
=	Indians	5
9 =	Royals	2
=	Blue Jays	2

The Athletics have won championships while based in Philadelphia and Oakland. They played in Kansas City from 1955–67, but didn't add to their total while there.

Most A.L. Championship Series Championships

	TEAM	ALCS TITLES
1	New York Yankees	10
2	Athletics	6
3	Orioles	5
4 =	Royals	2
=	Red Sox	2
=	Twins	2
=	Blue Jays	2
=	Indians	2
9 =	Brewers	1
=	Tigers	1

Since 1969, each league's champion has been the winner of the League Championship Series. Beginning in 1995, another round of playoffs, the Division Series, was added before the LCS.

MASCOT EARNS A'S
Stomper the Elephant works for peanuts.

Longest-Serving Team Owners

OWNER, TEAM, TIMESPAN	YEARS
1 = Phillip K. Wrigley, Cubs (1934–77)	43
= Thomas Yawkey, Red Sox (1933–76)	43
3 Horace Stoneham, Giants (1936–75)	39
4 = Gene Autry, Angels (1960–97)	37
= August Busch, Jr., Cardinals (1953–89)	36
6 Clark Griffith, Senators (1969–93)	35
7 Barney Dreyfuss, Pirates (1900–32)	32
8 George Steinbrenner, Yankees (1973–)	31
9 Charles Comiskey, White Sox (1901–31)	30
10 = Calvin Griffith, Senators/Twins (1956–84)	28
= Allan H. "Bud" Selig*, Brewers (1970–98)	28

Note: Selig left his position with the Brewers to become Commissioner of Baseball, having served as Interim Commissioner from 1993–98. If Wrigley sounds familiar, he's from the gum family.

Most N.L. Championships

TEAM	PENNANTS
1 Brooklyn/Los Angeles Dodgers	21
2 New York/San Francisco Giants	20
3 = Boston/Milwaukee/Atlanta Braves	17
3 Chicago Cubs	16
4 St. Louis Cardinals	15
5 = Pittsburgh Pirates	9
= Cincinnati Reds	9
8 Philadelphia Phillies	5
9 New York Mets	4
10 = San Diego Padres	2
= Florida Marlins	2

The Dodgers and Giants have one of baseball's oldest and fiercest rivalries. First, they battled for N.L. supremacy in New York. After both moving to the West Coast in 1958, the two clubs kept up the scrapping and maintained their rivalry. The Giants, however, have not won a Series title in the Bay Area, while the Dodgers have won five.

Most N.L. Championship Series Championships

TEAM	NLCS TITLES
1 = Los Angeles Dodgers	5
= Cincinnati Reds	5
= Atlanta Braves	5
4 New York Mets	4
5 = Philadelphia Phillies	3
= St. Louis Cardinals	3
7 = Pittsburgh Pirates	2
= San Diego Padres	2
= San Francisco Giants	2
= Florida Marlins	2

The Braves appeared in the eight National League Championship Series in a row from 1991–99 (no NLCS held in 1994).

THE GONFALON

You are a true baseball nut if you know the meaning of that term. It is an extremely archaic version of the word "pennant," and even when people knew what it meant, it was rarely used. The pennant, of course, is the synonym for a league championship, after the huge flag once given to winners. Derived from the Italian word for flag, *gonfalone*, it would have disappeared into obscurity if not for a poem. In the poem, 1908 Cubs infielders Joe Tinker, Johnny Evers, and Frank Chance are lauded for their double-play ability. The poem claims that the famous trio are "…fearlessly pricking our gonfalon bubble."

SNAP SHOTS

DID YOU KNOW?
The Arizona Diamondbacks made it to the World Series in only their fourth season, the fastest-ever trip to the Fall Classic by an expansion team.

55

TEAMS AROUND THE WORLD

International Homes of Major Leaguers

	COUNTRY OF ORIGIN	PLAYERS
1	**Dominican Republic**	79
2	**Puerto Rico**	38
3	**Venezuela**	37
4	**Mexico**	17
5	**Japan**	11
6=	**Canada**	10
=	**Cuba**	10
7	**Panama**	7
8	**Korea**	6
9=	**Australia**	3
=	**Colombia**	3

More and more players from more and more countries are flocking to the Major Leagues. For the 2003 season, nearly 28 percent of Major Leaguers were born outside the United States, the highest percentage ever. This list reflects a ranking of the total numbers of players on 2003 Opening Day rosters from each country.

Recent Caribbean World Series Champs

	TEAM, COUNTRY	YEAR
1	**Aguilas,** Dominican Republic	2003
2	**Culiacan**, Mexico	2002
3	**Aguilas,** Dominican Republic	2001
4	**Santurce**, Puerto Rico	2000
5	**Licey,** Dominican Republic	1999
6	**Aguilas**, Dominican Republic	1998
7	**Aguilas,** Dominican Republic	1997
8	**Culiacan**, Mexico	1996
9	**San Juan**, Puerto Rico	1995
10	**Licey**, Dominican Republic	1994

The Caribbean Series is played in the winter among league-champion clubs from Caribbean and Latin American teams. Many Major Leaguers play on these teams during their winter break.

Recent Mexican League Champions

	TEAM	YEAR
1	**Mexico City Diablos Rojos**	2002
2	**Mexico City Tigres**	2001
3	**Mexico City Tigres**	2000
4	**Mexico City Diablos Rojos**	1999
5	**Oaxaca Guerreros**	1998
6	**Mexico City Tigres**	1997
7	**Monterrey Sultanes**	1996
8	**Monterrey Sultanes**	1995
9	**Mexico City Diablos Rojos**	1994
10	**Villahermosa Olmecas**	1993

Mexico's pro league, formed in 1925, has 16 teams playing in the winter months. In recent years, stars such as slugging third baseman Vinny Castilla have joined a long list of Mexican players making an impact on the Major Leagues. Historical note: In the 1940s, the Mexican league fought an ultimately losing salary war with the Major Leagues, convincing several top stars to leave their U.S. teams and play in Mexico.

K IS FOR KOREA

While with the Dodgers in 2001, fireballing righthander Chan Ho Park earned the first All-Star selection for a Korean-born player.

THE TOP 10

Most Japan Series Championships

	TEAM	CHAMPIONSHIPS
1	Yomiuri Giants	20
2	Seibu Lions	11
3	Yakult Swallows	5
4=	Hankyu Braves	3
=	Hiroshima Carp	3
6=	Nankai Hawks	2
=	Manichi/Lotte Orions	2
8	Six teams are tied with 1 championship each	

The Japanese professional league began in 1936. Today six teams play in each of the Central and Pacific Leagues; since 1950, their champions oppose each other in the postseason Japan Series. With their near-complete domination of the sport in Japan, the Yomiuri (Tokyo) Giants are the Yankees of Japanese baseball. Recently, stars such as Ichiro Suzuki, Hideo Nomo, and Kazuhiro Sasaki have moved from Japan to the U.S.

THE TOP 10

Recent Japan Series Champs

	TEAM	YEAR
1	Fukuoka Daiei Hawks	2003
2	Yomiuri Giants	2002
3	Yakult Swallows	2001
4	Yomiuri Giants	2000
5	Fukuoka Daiei Hawks	1999
6	Yokohama Bay Stars	1998
7	Yakult Swallows	1997
8	Orix Blue Wave	1996
9	Yakult Swallows	1995
10	Yomiuri Giants	1994

THE TOP 10

Recent Korean League Champions

	TEAM	TITLES
1	Samsung Lions	2002
2	Doosan Bears	2001
3	Hyundai Unicorns	2000
4	Hanwha Eagles	1999
5	Hyundai Unicorns	1998
6	Haitai Tigers	1997
7	Haitai Tigers	1996
8	OB Bears	1995
9	LG Twins	1994
10	Haitai Tigers	1993

Korean pro baseball began in 1982 with the formation of the Korean Baseball Organization. The Tigers have won the most (9 of 19 through 1998) KBO titles. Dodgers pitcher Chan Ho Park is the most noted Korean player to join the Major Leagues, but several other players are training in the minors for their MLB debuts.

THE TOP 10

Recent Australian Baseball League Champions

	TEAM	SEASON
1	Queensland Rams	2002–03
2	Victorian Aces	2001–02
3	Western Heelers	1999–2000
4	Gold Coast Cougars	1998–99
5	Melbourne Reds	1997–98
6	Perth Heat	1996–97
7	Sydney Blues	1995–96
8	Waverly Reds	1994–95
9	Brisbane Bandits	1993–94
10	Melbourne Monarchs	1992–93

Pro baseball is a fairly recent entrant on the busy Australian sports scene. There was an inter-state series called the Claxton Shield played from 1934–89, but a true pro league didn't start until 1989. Major Leaguers such as former Dodgers pitcher Luke Prokopec, former Brewers catcher Dave Nilsson, and Royals pitcher Graeme Lloyd hail from Down Under.

WORD PLAY
Many Major League teams broadcast in Spanish, but only the Montreal Expos go on the air in French. Listen for "frappeur" (batter), "lanceur" (pitcher), and "coups sûrs" (runs).

57

The Ten Most Recent Pan American Games Champions
(Team Championships)

❶ Cuba, 2003 **❷ Cuba**, 1999
❸ Cuba, 1995 **❹ Cuba**, 1991 **❺ Cuba**, 1987 **❻ Cuba**, 1983 **❼ Cuba**, 1979
❽ Cuba, 1975 **❾ Cuba**, 1971
❿ United States, 1967

The Pan Am Games began in 1951 as athletic competitions among the nations of North, South, and Central America. They are held every four years at different sites throughout the Western hemisphere. But it doesn't matter where they're held—Cuba always seems to win!

GOLD FOR CUBA
Omar Linares and Orestes Kindelan of the Cuban baseball team celebrate their 1996 gold medal. Cuba's national teams have dominated international competition.

2001 ERA Leaders Among Foreign-Born Players

	PLAYER (BORN IN…)	ERA
1	**Pedro Martinez** (Dom. Rep.)	2.22
2	**Esteban Loaiza** (Mexico)	2.90
3	**Hideo Nomo** (Japan)	3.09
4	**Carlos Zambrano** (Venezuela)	3.11
5	**Livan Hernandez** (Cuba)	3.20
6	**Javier Vazquez** (Puerto Rico)	3.24
7	**Miguel Batista** (Dom. Rep.)	3.54
8	**Vicente Padilla** (Nicaragua)	3.62
9	**Joel Pineiro** (Puerto Rico)	3.78
10	**Jae Weong Seo** (South Korea)	3.82

2003 B.A. Leaders Among Foreign-Born Players

	PLAYER (NATIVE COUNTRY)	BATTING AVERAGE
1	**Albert Pujols** (Dom. Rep.)	.359
2	**Edgar Renteria** (Columbia)	.330
3	**Manny Ramirez** (Dom. Rep.)	.325
4	**Magglio Ordonez** (Venezuela)	.317
5	**Luis Castillo** (Dom. Rep.)	.314
6	**Ichiro Suzuki** (Japan)	.312
7	**Jose Vidro** (Puerto Rico)	.310
8	**Richard Hidalgo** (Venezuela)	.309
9	**Carlos Beltran** (Puerto Rico)	.307
10	**Carlos Delgado** (Puerto Rico)	.302

All-Time Olympic Baseball Champions

	NATION	YEAR
1	**United States**	2000
2	**Cuba**	1996
3	**Cuba**	1992
4	**Japan**	1988
5	**Japan**	1984

Baseball has been an official medal sport in the Olympics only since 1988. In 1984 it was a "demonstration" sport, though medals were awarded. The baseball tournament proved to be so popular that it was added to the Olympic menu. In addition, baseball was played as a demonstration sport in 1956, in Melbourne, when a record 114,000 people watched a game. The first appearance of baseball in the Olympics was in 1924, in Paris. Many former Olympians now play in the Majors.

GAMES

TRIUMPHANT RIDE

In 1999, David Cone of the Yankees was the most recent player to achieve the greatest single-game feat by a pitcher: throwing a perfect game.

INNINGS AND TIMES

Longest Games by Number of Innings

TEAMS (SCORE), DATE	INNINGS
1 Dodgers 1–Braves 1, 5/1/20	26
2= Cardinal 4–Mets 2, 9/11/74	25
= White Sox 7–Brewers 6, 5/8/84	25
4= Athletics 4–Red Sox 1, 9/1/06	24
= Tigers 1–Athletics 1, 7/21/45	24
= Astros 1–Mets 0, 4/25/68	24
7= Dodgers 2–Braves 2, 6/27/39	23
= Giants 8–Mets 6, 5/31/64	23
9 Eight games took	22

One of the great things about baseball is that there is no clock. These are the games that just didn't want to end. (Note: In the days before lighted stadiums, games could end in ties, such as when games were occasionally called on account of darkness.)

Shortest Games by Time

TEAMS (YEAR)	TIME
1 Giants–Athletics (1919)	:51
2 Yankees–Browns (1926)	:55
3 Giants–Dodgers (1918)	:57
4= Phillies–Reds (1916)	:58
= Cubs–Braves (1919)	:58
6 Braves–Phillies (1920)	1:05
7= White Sox–Red Sox (1926)	1:07
= Dodgers–Cubs (1919)	1:07
9 Dodgers–Cubs (1919)	1:10
10 Cubs–Dodgers (1908)	1:12

A baseball game today normally clocks in at around three hours. But in the early days of baseball, games were played much more briskly. This list gathered from a book called *The Baseball Chronology* shows that that all the quick games were played long ago.

RECORD BREAKER
The October 5, 2001, game between the Giants and Dodgers was doubly special: It was the longest nine-inning game ever, and Barry Bonds (below) slugged his record-breaking 71st home run.

DID YOU KNOW?
In 1908, hard-luck pitcher Hooks Wiltse lost his chance at a perfect game when he hit the 27th batter with a pitch! The batter was the opposing pitcher!

THE TOP 10

Longest 9-Inning Games, by Time*

	TIME	TEAMS (SCORE)	DATE
1	**4 hours, 27 minutes**	Dodgers 11–Giants 10	10/5/01
2	**4 hours, 22 minutes**	Brewers 14–Cubs 8	5/11/00
=	**4 hours, 22 minutes**	Orioles 13–Yankees 9	9/5/97
4=	**4 hours, 21 minutes**	Rangers 14–Indians 7	8/31/00
=	**4 hours, 21 minutes**	Yankees 13–Orioles 10	4/30/96
6=	**4 hours, 20 minutes**	Tigers 14–White Sox 12	4/5/97
=	**4 hours, 20 minutes**	Orioles 14–Mariners 13	5/17/96
=	**4 hours, 20 minutes**	Rockies 16–Dodgers 15	6/30/96
9	**4 hours, 19 minutes**	Rockies 14–Cardinals 13	4/16/00
10	**4 hours, 16 minutes**	Orioles 18–Yankees 9	6/8/86

Lots of runs means lots of extra at-bats and lots of pitching changes. And all that means more time for fans and players at the ballpark (and that's not all bad, is it?). The longest nine-inning game ever came at the end of the 2001 season. A full house at Pacific Bell Park in San Francisco watched Barry Bonds of the Giants set a new single-season home run record with his 71st round-tripper. For good measure, he added his 72nd in that game as well. So that meant not only more runs, but more curtain calls for Bonds! (*Since 1981.)

THE TOP 10

Nearly Perfect Games

	PITCHER, TEAM (OPPONENT)	INNINGS	YEAR
1	**Harvey Haddix, Pirates** (Braves)	13	1959
2	**Pedro Martinez, Expos*** (Padres)	9	2001
3=	**Mike Mussina, Yankees*** (Red Sox	$8^2/_3$	2001
=	**Brian Holman, Athletics** (Mariners)	$8^2/_3$	1990
=	**Dave Stieb, Blue Jays** (Yankees)	$8^2/_3$	1989
=	**Ron Robinson, Reds** (Expos)	$8^2/_3$	1988
=	**Milt Wilcox, Tigers** (White Sox)	$8^2/_3$	1983
=	**Milt Pappas, Cubs** (Padres)	$8^2/_3$	1972
=	**Billy Pierce, White Sox** (Senators)	$8^2/_3$	1958
=	**Tommy Bridges, Tigers** (Senators)	$8^2/_3$	1932
=	**Hooks Wiltse, Giants** (Phillies)	$8^2/_3$	1908

Sixteen pitchers have completed baseball's rarest feat, the perfect game (see page 64). However, this list includes pitchers who carried perfect games into the ninth inning, and even into extra innings, before giving up a hit or walk to break up the "perfecto." The saddest case was Haddix, who retired a record 36 straight Milwaukee hitters before losing the game in the 13th inning.

THE TOP 10

Longest Extra-Inning Games, by Time*

	TIME	TEAMS, SCORE (INNINGS)	DATE
1	**8 hours, 6 minutes**	White Sox 7–Brewers 6 (25)	5/8/84
2	**7 hours, 14 minutes**	Astros 5–Dodgers 4 (22)	10/18/89
3	**6 hours, 36 minutes**	Indians 10–Twins 9 (17)	5/7/95
4	**6 hours, 35 minutes**	Rangers 8–Red Sox 7 (18)	8/25/01
5	**6 hours, 30 minutes**	Red Sox 7–Indians 5 (19)	4/11/92
6	**6 hours, 28 minutes**	Royals 4–Rangers 3 (18)	6/6/91
7	**6 hours, 17 minutes**	Twins 5–Indians 4 (22)	8/31/93
8	**6 hours, 14 minutes**	Dodgers 1–Expos 0 (22)	8/23/89
9=	**6 hours, 10 minutes**	Phillies 7–Dodgers 6 (20)	7/7/93
=	**6 hours, 10 minutes**	Mets 16–Braves 13 (19)	7/4/85
=	**6 hours, 10 minutes**	Dodgers 2–Cubs 1 (21)	8/17/82

Extra-inning games usually take longer than nine-inning games, but these games just kept going and going and going. One memorable postseason game that nearly made this list was the amazing 1999 NLCS game between the Braves and Mets. The Mets won in the 15th inning on Robin Ventura's "grand single. " He hit a home run with the bases loaded in the bottom of the 15th but never made it around the bases, since his teammates poured onto the field to celebrate, Ventura only got credit for a single. (*Since 1981.)

OH, SO CLOSE

A dejected Mike Mussina watches a single by Carl Everett of Boston land in the outfield. Mussina had retired the first 26 Red Sox batters in a row before Everett broke up the perfect game.

*Active through 2003

Most Hits by a Team in One Game

	TEAM, OPPONENT	DATE	HITS
1	**Cleveland** vs. **Philadelphia** (AL) July 10, 1932 (18 inn.)		33
2	**New York** (NL) vs. **Cincinnati**	June 9, 1901	31
3=	**New York** (NL) vs. **Philadelphia**	Sept. 2, 1925	30
=	**New York** (AL) vs. **Boston**	Sept. 28, 1923	30
5=	**Philadelphia** (AL) vs. **Boston**	May 1, 1929	29
=	**Cleveland** vs. **St. Louis** (AL)	Aug. 12, 1948	29
=	**Chicago** (AL) vs. **Kansas City**	April 23, 1955	29
=	**Oakland** vs. **Texas**	July 1, 1979 (15 inn.)	29
9	Many times; most recent: **New York** (NL) vs. **Atlanta**	July 4, 1985 (19 inn.)	28

With the all-time record in this category coming in an extra-inning game, perhaps the Giants' 31-hit attack in only nine innings in 1901 is worth a look. That's an average of more than three hits per inning. The Giants were not exactly sluggers that season; they finished 37 games out of first that year with one of the lowest team averages in the N.L. However, the opposing Reds had the league's highest ERA and gave up the most hits. Nice timing!

Most Runs by a Team in One Game

	TEAM, OPPONENT	DATE	RUNS
1=	**Boston** vs. **St. Louis**	June 8, 1950	29
=	**Chicago** (AL) vs. **Kansas City**	April 23, 1955	29
3	**St. Louis** vs. **Philadelphia** (NL)	July 6, 1929	28
4	**Cleveland** vs. **Boston**	July 7, 1923	27
5=	**Cincinnati** vs. **Boston**	June 4, 1911	26
=	**Chicago** (NL) vs. **Philadelphia** (NL)	Aug. 25, 1922	26
=	**New York** (NL) vs. **Brooklyn**	April 30, 1944	26
=	**Cleveland** vs. **St. Louis**	Aug. 12, 1948	26
=	**Philadelphia** vs. **New York** (NL)	April 11, 1985	26
10	Several times; most recent: **New York** (NL) vs. **Philadelphia**	May 24, 1936	25

That the 1950 Red Sox racked up 29 runs is not too surprising. The team scored 1,027 runs on the season, fourth-most all-time and still the highest total since 1936. They led the Majors with a .302 team average and 1,665 hits. Walt Dropo set a rookie record with 144 runs batted in for the Sox that season.

Most Runs Scored by a Team in One Inning

	TEAM, OPPONENT, DATE	INNING	RUNS
1	**Chicago** (NL) vs. **Detroit**, Sept. 6, 1883	7th	18
2	**Boston** vs. **Detroit**, June 18, 1953	7th	17
3	**Boston** vs. **Baltimore**, June 18, 1894	1st	16
4=	**Hartford** vs. **New York** (NL), May 13, 1876	4th	15
=	**Brooklyn** vs. **Cincinnati**, May 21, 1952	1st	15
6=	**New York** (AL) vs. **Washington**, July 6, 1920	5th	14
=	**Chicago** (NL) vs. **Philadephia** (NL), Aug. 25, 1922	4th	14
=	**Boston** vs. **Philadelphia** (AL), July 4, 1948	7th	14
=	**Cleveland** vs. **Philadelphia** (AL), Sept. 21, 1950	1st	14
=	**Boston** vs. **Florida**, June 27, 2003	1st	14
11	13 runs have been scored in one inning 8 times; most recent: **Detroit** vs. **Texas**, Aug. 8, 2001	9th	13

Amazingly, the top entry above also represents the final score. Detroit's inability to add even one run in the seventh kept the game from setting the record for most runs in an inning by both teams. That record is 19, set by the Red Sox and Indians in 1977.

BILLY BALL

Not even Hall-of-Fame slugger Billy Williams of the Cubs could stop the expansion San Diego Padres from whitewashing Chicago 19–0 in 1969.

THE TOP 10

Most Recent "Ultimate" Grand Slams

	PLAYER, TEAM	YEAR
1	**Jason Giambi**, Yankees	2002
2	**Brian Giles**, Pirates	2001
3	**Chris Hoiles**, Orioles	1996
4	**Alan Trammell**, Tigers	1998
5	**Dick Schofield**, Angels	1986
6	**Phil Bradley**, Mariners	1985
7	**Buddy Bell**, Rangers	1984
8	**Bo Diaz**, Phillies	1983
9	**Roger Freed**, Cardinals	1979
10	**Ron Lolich**, Phil.	1973

Your team is down by three runs, it's your team's final at-bat, there are two outs, and the bases are loaded. Guess what? You're up. These are the ten most recent players to hit a game-winning grand slam in a situation just like that one.

THE TOP 10

Most Career Games with Two-Plus Home Runs

	PLAYER	GAMES
1	**Babe Ruth**	72
2	**Mark McGwire**	67
3	**Willie Mays**	63
4	**Hank Aaron**	62
5 =	**Barry Bonds***	61
=	**Sammy Sosa***	61
7	**Jimmie Foxx**	55
8	**Frank Robinson**	54
9 =	**Eddie Mathews**	49
=	**Mel Ott**	49
11 =	**Harmon Killebrew**	46
=	**Mickey Mantle**	46

DOUBLE DIPPING
One home run record that the Bambino still holds is most games with two-plus homers.

THE TOP 10

Most Strikeouts in a Nine-Inning Game

	PITCHER, TEAM	DATE	STRIKEOUTS
1 =	**Roger Clemens***, Boston Red Sox	4/29/86	20
=	**Roger Clemens***, Boston Red Sox	9/18/96	20
=	**Kerry Wood***, Chicago Cubs	5/6/98	20
=	**Randy Johnson***, Arizona Diamondbacks	5/8/01	20
4 =	**Steve Carlton**, St. Louis Cardinals	9/15/69	19
=	**Tom Seaver**, New York Mets	4/22/70	19
=	**Nolan Ryan**, California Angels	8/12/74	19
=	**David Cone***, New York Mets	10/6/91	19
=	**Randy Johnson***, Seattle Mariners	8/8/97	19
=	**Randy Johnson***, Seattle Mariners	6/24/97	19

Controversy erupted when Johnson struck out 20 in 2001. He got his 20th "K" in the ninth , but the game was not over (he didn't strike out any more batters). At first, it appeared he wouldn't get credit for tying the record, but baseball soon announced that he was officially the fourth player with 20 strikeouts in 9 innings of a game.

THE TOP 10

Most Lopsided Shutouts, since 1900

	WINNING TEAM, OPPONENT	DATE	SCORE
1	**Pittsburgh** vs. **Chicago** (NL)	Sept. 16, 1975	22–0
2 =	**New York** (AL) vs. **Philadelphia** (AL)	August 13, 1939	21–0
=	**Detroit** vs. **Cleveland**	Sept. 15, 1901	21–0
4 =	**Montreal** vs. **Atlanta**	July 30, 1978	19–0
=	**Los Angeles** vs. **San Diego**	June 28, 1969	19–0
=	**Chicago** (NL) vs. **San Diego**	May 13, 1969	19–0
=	**Pittsburgh** vs. **St. Louis**	Aug. 3, 1961	19–0
=	**Cleveland** vs. **Boston**	May 18, 1955	19–0
=	**Boston** vs. **Philadelphia** (AL)	April 30, 1950	19–0
=	**Chicago** (NL) vs. **New York** (NL)	June 7, 1906	19–0

Pittsburgh's smashing success over Chicago is only surprising in the total, not in the result. The Pirates won the NL East that year, while the Cubbies were 17.5 games back. Pittsburgh led the NL with 138 homers and a .402 slugging average. Chicago, meanwhile, brought up the rear in the league with a 4.50 ERA while surrendering a league-high 130 homers. Ouch.

* Active through 2003

QUIZ TIME
Everyone knows that David Cone pitched the most recent A.L. perfect game in 1999. But can you name the pitcher who threw the most recent N.L. "perfecto"? See page 64.

PERFECT GAMES

Most Recent No-Hitters by A.L. Pitchers

PITCHER, TEAM, SCORE	YEAR
1 **Derek Lowe***, Red Sox, 10–0	2002
2 **Hideo Nomo***, Red Sox, 3–0	2001
3 **Eric Milton***, Twins, 7–0	1999
4 **David Cone***, Yankees, 5–0#	1999
5 **David Wells***, Yankees, 4–0#	1998
6 **Dwight Gooden**, Yankees, 2–0	1996
7 **Kenny Rogers***, Rangers, 4–0#	1994
8 **Scott Erickson***, Twins, 6–0	1994
9 **Jim Abbott**, Yankees, 4–0	1993
10 **Chris Bosio**, Mariners, 7–0	1993

In 2001, Hideo Nomo became the third pitcher to win no-hitters in both leagues. *(#Designates a perfect game.)*

Most Recent No-Hitters by N.L. Pitchers

PITCHER, TEAM, SCORE	YEAR
1 **Roy Oswalt***/Peter Munro*/ Kirk Saarloos*/Brad Lidge*/ Octavio Dotel*/Billy Wagner***, Astros, 8–0	2003
2 **Kevin Millwood***, Phillies, 1–0	2003
3 **Bud Smith**, Cardinals, 4–0	2001
4 **A. J. Burnett***, Marlins, 3–0	2001
5 **Jose Jimenez***, Cardinals, 1–0	1999
6 **Francisco Cordova***/Ricardo Rincon***, Pirates 3–0	1997
7 **Kevin Brown***, Marlins, 9–0	1997
8 **Hideo Nomo***, Dodgers, 9–0	1996
9 **Al Leiter***, Marlins, 11–0	1996
10 **Ramon Martinez**, Dodgers, 7–0	1995

Most Recent Perfect Games

PITCHER, TEAM	DATE
1 **David Cone**, Yankees	7/18/99
2 **David Wells**, Yankees	5/17/98
3 **Kenny Rogers**, Rangers	7/28/94
4 **Dennis Martinez**, Expos	7/28/91
5 **Tom Browning**, Reds	9/16/88
6 **Mike Witt**, Angels	9/30/84
7 **Len Barker**, Indians	5/15/81
8 **Catfish Hunter**, Athletics	5/8/68
9 **Sandy Koufax**, Dodgers	9/9/65
10 **Jim Bunning**, Phillies	6/21/64

A perfect game is baseball's rarest pitching feat. It has been accomplished only 16 times in baseball history, including only once during a World Series, by Don Larsen in 1956. Two of the "perfectos" were pitched in 1880, when underhand pitching from 45 feet away was the rule. To achieve the feat, a pitcher must retire all 27 batters he faces in a 9-inning game, and his team must score at least once to give him the win. In 1995, Pedro Martinez pitched 9 perfect innings, but his Montreal team had not scored, and he lost the perfect game in the 10th. In 1959, Pirates pitcher Harvey Haddix pitched 12 perfect innings in a 0–0 game until it was broken up in the 13th and he went on to lose.

Most Strikeouts in a Perfect Game
(Player/Strikeouts)

❶ **Sandy Koufax**, 14 ❷ **Catfish Hunter**, 11 = **Len Barker**, 11 = **Kenny Rogers***, 11 = **David Wells***, 11 ❻ **Jim Bunning**, 10 = **Mike Witt**, 10 = **David Cone**, 10 ❾ **Cy Young**, 8 ❿ **Don Larsen**, 7 = **Tom Browning**, 7

ON TOP OF THE WORLD

David Cone is carried off the field on the shoulders of his Yankees teammates after he threw a perfect game in 1999.

* Active through 2003

WORLD SERIES

THE FALL CLASSIC
Reggie Jackson's 3 home runs in one game in the 1977 World Series is one of many outstanding performances by baseball's biggest stars on the game's biggest stage.

CASEY'S BOYS

The Yankees under manager Casey Stengel (center) had a lot of practice celebrating. They won seven World Series titles in 10 seasons from 1949–58. They also played in and lost the 1955 and 1957 Series, adding to the Yankees' outstanding all-time record in World Series play.

THE TOP 10

Longest Time Since Last World Series Championship

	FRANCHISE	MOST RECENT TITLE	YEARS SINCE
1	Chicago Cubs	1908	95
2	Chicago White Sox	1917	86
3	Boston Red Sox	1918	85
4	Cleveland Indians	1948	55
5	New York/San Francisco Giants	1954	49
6	Pittsburgh Pirates	1979	24
7	Philadelphia Phillies	1980	23
8	St. Louis Cardinals	1982	21
9	St. Louis Browns/Baltimore Orioles	1983	20
10	Detroit Tigers	1984	19

In 1920, Boston owner Harry Frazee sold Babe Ruth to the New York Yankees for money to finance a Broadway play Frazee wanted to produce. The Sox have not won a Series since, and many say the reason is "The Curse of the Bambino," thanks to Frazee's folly. The Sox came within one strike of winning in 1986, but managed to blow it. They also had the lead in two Game 7s, but the Curse of the Bambino foiled them yet again.

THE TOP 10

All-time Best World Series Winning Percentage

	TEAM	W	L	APPEARANCES	PCT.
1=	Toronto Blue Jays	2	0	2	1.000
=	Florida Marlins	2	0	2	1.000
=	Arizona Diamondbacks	1	0	1	1.000
=	Anaheim Angels	1	0	1	1.000
5	Pittsburgh Pirates	5	2	7	.714
6	New York Yankees	26	13	39	.667
7	Philadelphia/Kansas City/Oakland A's	9	5	14	.643
8	St. Louis Cardinals	9	6	15	.600
9=	Cincinnati Reds	5	4	9	.556
=	Boston Red Sox	5	4	9	.556

This list ranks annual World Series appearances, not individual World Series games. For instance, the Blue Jays and Marlins have appeared in two Series and won them both (most recently the Marlins in 2003). The Yankees remarkable success over the past 100 years of World Series play is shown by these numbers. They have actually *lost* more World Series than any other team has *won*! Their 39 appearances are more than twice the Cardinals' 15!

THE HARDWARE

While players receive individual World Series rings, the team is given this official Major League Baseball World Series Championship Trophy. Redesigned before the 2000 season, the sterling-silver base features red baseball stitching. The thirty vertical stainless steel poles are each topped with a pennant that represents a Major League team. In recent years, the ceremony in which the Commissioner presents the trophy to the winning team owner and manager has moved from the crowded, noisy locker room onto a platform that is erected on the field moments after the final out, so that all the fans can share in the most special moment in baseball.

SNAP SHOTS

Teams That Have Never Won the World Series

	FRANCHISE	FIRST SEASON	LAST W.S. APP.
1	Washington Senators/ Texas Rangers	1961	—-
2	Houston Astros	1962	—-
3=	Montreal Expos	1969	—-
=	Seattle Pilots/Milwaukee Brewers	1969	1982
=	San Diego Padres	1969	1998
6	Seattle Mariners	1977	—-
7	Colorado Rockies	1993	—-
8	Tampa Bay Devil Rays	1998	—-

Most Recent W.S. Champs and MVPs

YEAR	TEAM (MVP)
2003	**Florida Marlins** (Josh Beckett*)
2002	**Anaheim Angels** (Troy Glaus*)
2001	**Arizona Diamondbacks** (Curt Schilling* and Randy Johnson*)
2000	**New York Yankees** (Derek Jeter*)
1999	**New York Yankees** (Mariano Rivera*)
1998	**New York Yankees** (Scott Brosius)
1997	**Florida Marlins** (Livan Hernandez*)
1996	**New York Yankees** (John Wetteland)
1995	**Atlanta Braves** (Tom Glavine*)
1993	**Toronto Blue Jays** (Paul Molitor)

Note: The 1994 World Series was not played due to a labor dispute between players and owners that ended the season on August 12 of that year.

SURPRISE MVP

In only their fifth season, the Florida Marlins, led by pitcher Livan Hernandez, stunned baseball by winning the World Series, defeating the Cleveland Indians.

First Ten W.S. Champions

	TEAM	YEAR
1	Boston Americans	1903
2	New York Giants	1905
3	Chicago White Sox	1906
4	Chicago Cubs	1907
5	Chicago Cubs	1908
6	Pittsburgh Pirates	1909
7	Philadelphia Athletics	1910
8	Philadelphia Athletics	1911
9	Boston Red Sox	1912
10	Philadephia Athletics	1913

The New York Giants refused to play the American League champion Boston Pilgrims after the 1904 season, saying that the newer "junior" circuit was not worthy. The Series resumed in 1905, uninterrupted until 1994.

* Active through 2003

WORLD SERIES BATTING

Most Home Runs, W.S. Career

	PLAYER	HOME RUNS
1	Mickey Mantle	18
2	Babe Ruth	15
3	Yogi Berra	12
4	Duke Snider	11
5=	Reggie Jackson	10
=	Lou Gehrig	10
7=	Frank Robinson	8
=	Bill Skowron	8
=	Joe DiMaggio	8
10	Goose Goslin	7
=	Hank Bauer	7
=	Gil McDougald	7

YER OUT!

Yogi Berra, who played in more World Series games than any other player, tags out a sliding Granny Hamner of the Phillies in Game 3 of the 1950 World Series.

Most W.S. Runs Batted In, Career

	PLAYER	RBI
1	Mickey Mantle	40
2	Yogi Berra	39
3	Lou Gehrig	35
4	Babe Ruth	33
5	Joe DiMaggio	30
6	Bill Skowron	29
7	Duke Snider	26
8	Reggie Jackson	24
8	Bill Dickey	24
8	Hank Bauer	24
8	Gil McDougald	24

The Yankees have played in and won more World Series than any other team, so it's no surprise that they dominate the career batting lists. In fact, of these RBI leaders, only Duke Snider of the Brooklyn Dodgers never played for the Yankees. Jackson, of course, also recorded RBI for the Oakland Athletics, whom he helped win three Series.

Most W.S. Hits, Career

	PLAYER	HITS
1	Yogi Berra	71
2	Mickey Mantle	59
3	Frankie Frisch	58
4	Joe DiMaggio	54
5=	Pee Wee Reese	46
=	Hank Bauer	46
7=	Phil Rizzuto	45
=	Gil McDougald	45
9	Lou Gehrig	43
10=	Eddie Collins	42
=	Babe Ruth	42
=	Elston Howard	42

In his career from 1946 to 1965, Yankees catcher and outfielder Berra played in 14 World Series, winning 10. He later went on to manage the Mets and the Yankees, and was as famous for his unusual sayings as his batting prowess. His most famous phrase was, "It ain't over 'til it's over."

LISTEN HERE, KID
Centerfielder Mickey Mantle (right) was a part of five of manager Casey Stengel's seven World Series-winning teams.

THE TOP 10

Most W.S. Career Runs Scored

	PLAYER	RUNS
1	Mickey Mantle	42
2	Yogi Berra	41
3	Babe Ruth	37
4	Lou Gehrig	30
5=	Joe DiMaggio	27
=	Derek Jeter*	27
7	Roger Maris	26
8	Elston Howard	25
9	Gil McDougald	23
10	Jackie Robinson	22

Jeter added five more runs scored during the 2003 World Series. He has scored in six different World Series, thanks to the Yankees' outstanding record in recent years. One of his runs came on his game-winning 10th-inning home run that won Game 4 in the 2001 World Series.

THE TOP 10

Highest Career World Series Batting Average#

	PLAYER	AVERAGE
1=	Paul Molitor	.418
=	Pepper Martin	.418
3	Lou Brock	.391
4	Marquis Grissom*	.390
5=	George Brett	.373
=	Thurman Munson	.373
7	Hank Aaron	.364
8	Frank Baker	.363
9	Roberto Clemente	.362
10	Lou Gehrig	.361

Minimum 50 at bats

Pepper Martin had one of baseball's coolest nicknames: "Wild Horse of the Osage."

THE TOP 10

Most Career World Series Stolen Bases

	PLAYER	STEALS
1=	Lou Brock	14
=	Eddie Collins	14
3=	Frank Chance	10
=	Davey Lopes	10
=	Phil Rizzuto	10
6=	Honus Wagner	9
=	Frankie Frisch	9
=	Kenny Lofton*	9
9	Johnny Evers	8
10=	Five players tied with	7

THE TOP 10

Most Career World Series Games Played

	PLAYER	GAMES
1	Yogi Berra	75
2	Mickey Mantle	65
3	Elston Howard	54
4=	Hank Bauer	53
=	Gil McDougald	53
6	Phil Rizzuto	52
7	Joe DiMaggio	51
8	Frankie Frisch	50
9	Pee Wee Reese	44
10=	Roger Maris	41
=	Babe Ruth	41

Frankie Frisch, the "Fordham Flash," played in eight World Series for the Giants and Cardinals from 1919–1937.

*Active through 2003

QUIZ TIME
Mickey Mantle leads in career Series home runs. Can you name the Yankees slugger who holds the record for most home runs in a single World Series? Answer on page 70.

69

BATTING RECORDS

MR. OCTOBER

Reggie Jackson called himself "the straw that stirred the drink" of the great Yankee teams of the late 1970s. He earned another nickname, Mr. October, for his clutch hitting in the World Series. In Game 6 of the 1977 World Series, he was Mr. One for the Ages. Jackson lined the first pitch he saw in the fourth inning for a two-run homer. With two out in the fifth, he again hit the first pitch thrown to him into the seats. In the eighth, with New York leading 7–3 and only three outs away from a World Series title, Jackson smashed the first pitch for his record-tying third homer.

SNAP SHOTS

THE TOP 10

Most Hits, Single World Series

PLAYER, SERIES (NUMBER OF GAMES)	HITS
1= **Bobby Richardson**, 1964 (7)	13
= **Lou Brock**, 1968 (7)	13
= **Marty Barrett**, 1986 (7)	13
4= **Billy Martin**, 1953 (6)	12
= **Roberto Alomar***, 1993 (6)	12
= **Paul Molitor**, 1993 (6)	12
= **Marquis Grissom***, 1996 (6)	12
8= **Sam Rice**, 1925 (7)	12
= **Pepper Martin**, 1931 (7)	12
= **Bill Skowron**, 1960 (7)	12
= **Lou Brock**, 1967 (7)	12
= **Roberto Clemente**, 1971 (7)	12
= **Phil Garner**, 1979 (7)	12
= **Willie Stargell**, 1979 (7)	12
= **Robin Yount**, 1982 (7)	12

In 1912, Buck Herzog racked up 12 hits, while Joe Jackson did the same in 1919. In both years, the Series went 8 games.

THE TOP 10

Highest Single-Series World Series Batting Average#

	PLAYER, YEAR	AVERAGE
1	**Billy Hatcher**, 1990	.750
2	**Babe Ruth**, 1928	.625
3	**Ricky Ledee***, 1998	.600
4	**Danny Bautista***, 2001	.583
5	**Chris Sabo**, 1990	.562
6	**Hank Gowdy**, 1914	.545
7	**Lou Gehrig**, 1928	.545
8	**Bret Boone***, 1999	.538
9	**Deion Sanders**, 1992	.533
10	**Johnny Bench**, 1976	.533

 # Minimum 10 at bats

All of these players reached these marks in 4-game World Series, except for Bautista, who had 7 hits in 12 at bats while playing in 5 games of Arizona's 7-game victory and Sanders, whose .533 was the best average in a 6-game Series.

THE TOP 10

Highest Batting Average in a 7-Game World Series#

	PLAYER, YEAR	AVERAGE
1	**Phil Garner**, 1979	.500
2	**Johnny Lindell**, 1947	.500
3	**Pepper Martin**, 1931	.500
4	**Tim McCarver**, 1964	.478
5	**Barry Bonds***, 2002	.471
6	**Lou Brock**, 1968	.464
7	**Max Carey**, 1925	.458
8	**Joe Harris**, 1925	.440
9	**Tony Perez**, 1972	.435
10	**Marty Barrett**, 1986	.433

 # Minimum 21 plate appearances

This list features the players who were most successful over the course of the longest Series possible (excluding the rare 8-game Series early in the 20th century). Both Martin and Garner had 12 hits in 24 at-bats.

THE TOP 10

Most Stolen Bases in a Single World Series

PLAYER, YEAR (NO. OF GAMES)	STOLEN BASES
1= **Lou Brock**, 1967 (7)	7
= **Lou Brock**, 1968 (7)	7
3= **Jimmy Slagle**, 1907 (5)	6
= **Honus Wagner**, 1909 (7)	6
= **Vince Coleman**, 1987 (7)	6
= **Kenny Lofton***, 1995 (6)	6
7= **Six players tied with**	5

Most recent: , **Omar Vizquel***, 1997 (7)

Lou Brock was one of the greatest base stealers of all time. When he retired in 1979, his 938 steals were the most all-time. He also held the single-season mark with 118 in 1974.

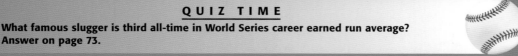

QUIZ TIME
What famous slugger is third all-time in World Series career earned run average?
Answer on page 73.

THE TOP 10

Most Runs Batted in a Single World Series

PLAYER, YEAR (NO. OF GAMES)	RBI
1 Bobby Richardson, 1960 (7)	12
2 Mickey Mantle, 1960 (7)	11
3 = Sandy Alomar, Jr.*, 1997 (7)	10
= Ted Kluszewski, 1959 (6)	10
= Yogi Berra, 1956 (7)	10
6 = Danny Murphy, 1910 (5)	9
= Lou Gehrig, 1928 (4)	9
= Moises Alou*, 1997 (7)	9
= Tony Fernandez, 1993 (6)	9
= Gary Carter, 1986 (7)	9
= Dwight Evans, 1986 (7)	9
= Gene Tenace, 1972 (7)	9

Bobby Richardson was a solid second baseman for the Yankees who had surprising success during the 1960 Series, which the Yankees lost to Pittsburgh.

THE TOP 10

Most Home Runs in a Single World Series

PLAYER, YEAR (# GAMES IN SERIES)	HOME RUNS
1 Reggie Jackson, 1977 (6)	5
2 = Willie Aikens, 1980 (6)	4
= Lenny Dykstra, 1993 (6)	4
= Lou Gehrig, 1928 (4)	4
= Hank Bauer, 1958 (7)	4
= Babe Ruth, 1926 (7)	4
= Duke Snider, 1952 (7)	4
= Duke Snider, 1955 (7)	4
= Gene Tenace, 1972 (7)	4
= Barry Bonds*, 2002 (7)	4

Donn Clendenon of the Mets hit 3 home runs in 1969, the most in a 5-game Series.

Active through 2003

TENACE, ANYONE?

Catcher–first baseman Gene Tenace hit only 5 home runs in the 1972 season for Oakland, so no one expected much from him in the World Series against Cincinnati. But following in a long line of unlikely Series heroes, Tenace hit 4 home runs, had 9 RBI, and batted .348, helping the A's to a seven-game triumph, their first of three consecutive World Series titles.

PITCHING RECORDS

THE TOP 10

Lowest ERA, 7-Game Series*

	PITCHER, YEAR	ERA
1	Whitey Ford, 1960	0.00
2	Duster Mails, 1920	0.00
3	Sandy Koufax, 1965	0.38
4	Harry Brecheen, 1946	0.45
5	Wild Bill Hallahan, 1931	0.49
6	Bret Saberhagen*, 1985	0.50
7	Sherry Smith, 1920	0.53
8	Claude Osteen, 1965	0.64
9	Lew Burdette, 1957	0.67
10	Stan Coveleski, 1920	0.67

Minimum 14 innings pitched

A seven-game World Series is often among the most dramatic of baseball events. Starting pitchers are under enormous pressure, since they often are the linchpins of a team's success. In addition, they often have to pitch more often than they did during the regular season.

THE TOP 10

Most Career Wins

	PITCHER	WINS
1	Whitey Ford	10
2=	Bob Gibson	7
=	Red Ruffing	7
=	Allie Reynolds	7
5=	Lefty Gomez	6
=	Chief Bender	6
=	Waite Hoyt	6
8=	Jack Coombs	5
=	Mordecai Brown	5
=	Herb Pennock	5
=	Christy Mathewson	5
=	Vic Raschi	5
=	Catfish Hunter	5

Once again, Yankee ace Ford (right) sits atop the leaderboard; he helped New York win 6 Series in the 1950s and 1960s.

THE TOP 10

Most Career Strikeouts

	PITCHER	STRIKEOUTS
1	Whitey Ford	94
2	Bob Gibson	92
3	Allie Reynolds	62
4=	Sandy Koufax	61
=	Red Ruffing	61
6	Chief Bender	59
7	George Earnshaw	56
8	John Smoltz*	52
9	Waite Hoyt	49
10=	Christy Mathewson	48
=	Roger Clemens*	48

THE TOP 10

Most Games Pitched

	PITCHER	GAMES
1	Whitey Ford	22
2=	Mike Stanton*	20
=	Mariano Rivera*	20
4=	Rollie Fingers	16
=	Jeff Nelson*	16
6=	Allie Reynolds	15
=	Bob Turley	15
8	Clay Carroll	14
9=	Clem Labine	13
=	Mark Wohlers	13

QUIZ TIME

Consider yourself a baseball expert if you know which player played in the most career regular-season games without ever appearing in a World Series. See page 75.

THE TOP 10
Lowest Career ERA#

	PITCHER	ERA
1	Jack Billingham	0.36
2	Harry Brecheen	0.83
3	Babe Ruth	0.87
4	Sherry Smith	0.89
5	Sandy Koufax	0.95
6	Hippo Vaughn	1.00
7	Monte Pearson	1.01
8	Christy Mathewson	1.06
9	Mariano Rivera*	1.16
10	Babe Adams	1.29

Minimum 25 innings pitched

Koufax, Mathewson, Vaughn, even Harry "The Cat" Brecheen—you expect to see pitchers like that on this list. But Ruth? That's right—Before he became a slugging outfielder for the Yankees, Ruth was an ace pitcher for the Red Sox, helping them win World Series titles in 1915, 1916, and 1918. He once threw a record 29 scoreless World Series innings, a record not broken until Whitey Ford did it in 1961.

THE TOP 10
Most Wins, Single World Series

	PITCHER, YEAR (NO. OF GAMES)	WINS
1=	Christy Mathewson, 1905 (5)	3
=	Jack Coombs, 1910 (5)	3
=	Babe Adams, 1909 (7)	3
=	Stan Coveleski, 1920 (7)	3
=	Harry Brecheen, 1946 (7)	3
=	Lew Burdette, 1957 (7)	3
=	Bob Gibson, 1967 (7)	3
=	Mickey Lolich, 1968 (7)	3
=	Randy Johnson, 2001 (7)	3
=	Bill Dineen, 1903 (8)	3
=	Deacon Phillippe, 1903 (8)	3
=	Smokey Joe Wood, 1912 (8)	3
=	Red Faber, 1917 (6)	3

In 2001, fireballing lefthander Randy Johnson earned two of his wins as expected with his performances as a starting pitcher. But in Game 7, he came out of the bullpen to shut down the Yankees. When Arizona won in the bottom of the ninth, Johnson had his third victory of the Series.

THE TOP 10
Most Career Saves

	PITCHER	SAVES
1	Mariano Rivera*	9
2	Rollie Fingers	6
3=	Allie Reynolds	4
=	John Wetteland	4
=	Robb Nen*	4
=	Johnny Murphy	4
7=	Roy Face	3
=	Herb Pennock	3
=	Kent Tekulve	3
=	Firpo Marberry	3
=	Will McEnaney	3
=	Todd Worrell	3
=	Tug McGraw	3
=	Troy Percival*	3

A team that wins a lot of games in today's baseball needs a strong closer to shut the door on opponents in the ninth. On their way to four World Series titles in five years (1996–2000), the Yankees turned to Wetteland and Rivera. Wetteland saved all four New York victories in 1996, setting the record for most saves in a World Series.

THE TOP 10
Most Strikeouts in a Game

	PITCHER, TEAM (YEAR)	STRIKEOUTS	OPPONENT
1	Bob Gibson, St. Louis (1968)	17	Detroit
2	Sandy Koufax, Los Angeles (NL) (1963)	15	New York (AL)
3	Carl Erskine, Brooklyn (1953)	14	New York (AL)
4=	Bob Gibson, St. Louis (1964)	13	New York (AL) (10 inn.)
=	Howard Ehmke, Philadelphia (AL) (1929)	13	Chicago (NL)
6=	Walter Johnson, Washington (1924)	12	New York (NL)
=	Bill Donovan Detroit (1907)	12	Chicago (NL) (12 inn.)
=	Ed Walsh, Chicago (AL) (1906)	12	Chicago (NL)
=	Mort Cooper, St. Louis (NL) (1944)	12	St. Louis
=	Tom Seaver, New York (NL) (1973)	12	Oakland
=	Orlando Hernandez*, New York (AL) (2000)	12	New York (NL)

Gibson's 17 Ks came in a shutout, but the Cards lost the Series.

0.00

Perhaps the most remarkable single World Series performance ever by a pitcher came in 1905. New York Giants's hurler Christy Mathewson put on an unmatched display of control, power, and endurance. He started three of the five games in the Series, struck out 18 batters, and walked only one. All of his wins were shutouts, and Giants pitchers allowed no earned runs in the Series. Mathewson, renowned for his gentlemanly air, was one of the first players elected to the Hall of Fame, in 1936.

SNAP SHOTS

Active through 2003

THE TOP 10

Highest Attendance, Single World Series Game

	ATTENDANCE	STADIUM	YEAR, GAME
1	92,706	L.A. Coliseum	1959, Game 5
2	92,650	L.A. Coliseum	1959, Game 4
3	92,394	L.A. Coliseum	1959, Game 3
4	86,288	Cleveland Municipal	1948, Game 5
5	81,897	Cleveland Municipal	1948, Game 4
6	78,102	Cleveland Municipal	1954, Game 4
7	74,065	Yankee Stadium	1947, Game 6
8	73,977	Yankee Stadium	1956, Game 3
9	73,365	Yankee Stadium	1947, Game 1
10	71,787	Yankee Stadium	1952, Game 4

Before they moved into Dodger Stadium in 1962, the Dodgers played at the immense Los Angeles Coliseum, built to house the 1932 Olympics. Huge crowds filled the stadium to see their new hometown team deliver a World Series title.

CHAMPAGNE SHOWER
Surrounded by reporters, Pirates second baseman Bill Mazeroski celebrates the dramatic homer he hit in the bottom of the ninth inning to win Game 7 of the 1960 World Series.

THE TOP 10

Most Runs Scored by One Team, World Series Game

	TEAM, OPPONENT, DATE	RUNS
1	**New York Yankees** vs. **N.Y. Giants** 10/2/36	18
2=	**New York Yankees** vs. **Pittsburgh Pirates** 10/6/60	16
=	**San Francisco Giants** vs. **Anaheim Angels** 10/24/2002	16
4	**Toronto Blue Jays** vs. **Philadelphia Phillies** 10/20/93	15
5	**Arizona Diamondbacks** vs. **N.Y. Yankees** 11/03/2001	15
6=	**Philadelphia Phillies** vs. **Toronto Blue Jays** 10/20/93	14
=	**Florida Marlins** vs. **Cleveland Indians** 10/21/97	14
=	**Atlanta Braves** vs. **Minnesota Twins** 10/24/91	14
9=	**Nine teams tied with**	13

The most recent team to put up 13 runs was the Oakland Athletics in Game 3 of the 1989 Series. The start of that game had been delayed by 10 days due to an earthquake that struck the Bay Area on October 17, 1989, the original date for Game 3. It was the longest gap between Series games in history and marked the first interruption for anything other than weather.

THE TOP 10

Most Lopsided World Series Wins

	TEAM, SCORE	YEAR, GAME, MARGIN	
1	**New York** (AL) 18, **New York** (NL) 4	1936, Game 2	14
2=	**New York** (AL) 16, **Pittsburgh** (NL) 3	1960, Game 2	13
=	**Arizona** (NL) 15, **New York** (AL) 2	2001, Game 6	13
4=	**St. Louis** (NL) 13, **Milwaukee** (AL) 1	1982, Game 6	12
=	**Detroit** (AL) 13, **St. Louis** (NL) 1	1968, Game 6	12
=	**New York** (AL) 12, **Pittsburgh** (NL) 0	1960, Game 6	12
=	**New York** (AL) 13, **New York** (NL) 1	1951, Game 5	12
=	**San Francisco** (NL) 16, **Anaheim** (AL) 4	2002, Game 5	12
9=	**Atlanta** (NL) 12, **New York** (AL) 1	1996, Game 1	11
=	**Kansas City** (AL) 11, **St. Louis** (NL) 0	1985, Game 7	11
=	**Chicago** (AL) 11, **Los Angeles** (NL) 0	1959, Game 1	11
=	**St. Louis** (NL) 11, **Detroit** (AL) 0	1934, Game 7	11
=	**Philadelphia (**AL) 13, **New York** (NL) 2	1911, Game 6	11

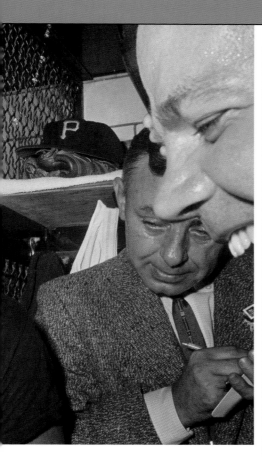

THE TOP 10
Highest Team Batting Average in a Series

	TEAM, YEAR	TEAM AVG.
1	**New York Yankees**, 1960	.338
2	**Pittsburgh Pirates**, 1979	.323
3	**Cincinnati Reds**, 1990	.317
4	**Philadelphia Athletics**, 1910	.316
5	**Cincinnati Reds**, 1976	.313
6	**New York Yankees**, 1932	.313
7	**Toronto Blue Jays**, 1993	.311
8	**New York Giants**, 1922	.309
9	**New York Yankees**, 1998	.309
10	**New York Yankees**, 1978	.306

The team with the best overall batting average in a World Series actually lost that Series! The Yankees outscored the Pirates 55–27 in seven games, but lost the Series in Game 7, 10–9, on Bill Mazeroski's famous homer in the bottom of the ninth inning.

THE TOP 10
Last 10 Players Who Hit Home Runs in their First World Series At-bat

	PLAYER, TEAM	YEAR
1	**Barry Bonds***, San Francisco	2002
2	**Troy Glaus***, Anaheim	2002
3	**Andruw Jones***, Atlanta	1996
4	**Fred McGriff***, Atlanta	1995
5	**Ed Sprague**, Toronto	1992
6	**Eric Davis**, Cincinnati	1990
7	**Bill Bathe**, San Francisco	1989
8	**Jose Canseco**, Oakland	1988
9	**Mickey Hatcher**, Los Angeles	1988
10	**Jim Dwyer**, Baltimore	1983

THE TOP 10
Most Games Played Without Playing in World Series

	PLAYER (SEASONS PLAYED)	GAMES
1	**Andre Dawson** (1976–96)	2,627
2	**Rafael Palmeiro*** (1986–)	2,567
3	**Ernie Banks** (1953–71)	2,528
4	**Billy Williams** (1959–76)	2,488
5	**Nap Lajoie** (1896–16)	2,480
6	**Rod Carew** (1967–85)	2,469
7	**Luke Appling** (1930–50)	2,422
8	**Mickey Vernon** (1939–60)	2,409
9	**Buddy Bell (**1972–89)	2,405
10	**Bobby Wallace** (1894–1918)	2,383

THE TOP 10
Most World Series Won by a Manager

1=	**Joe McCarthy**	7
=	**Casey Stengel**	7
3	**Connie Mack**	5
4=	**Walter Alston**	4
=	**Joe Torre**	4
6=	**Sparky Anderson**	3
=	**Miller Huggins**	3
=	**John McGraw**	3
9=	Eleven managers have led their teams to 2 titles	

George "Sparky" Anderson is the only manager to lead a team in both leagues to a Series title. He skippered the Reds in 1975 and 1976 and also ran the Tigers in 1984.

HEY, WE WON AGAIN!
Manager Joe McCarthy was blessed to lead teams with a little bit of talent...a couple of guys named Ruth and Gehrig.

*Active through 2003

LEAGUE CHAMPIONSHIP SERIES

THE TOP 10

Most Recent ALCS results

YEAR	TEAMS WITH GAMES WON
2003	Yankees 4, Red Sox 3
2002	Angels 4, Twins 1
2001	Yankees 4, Mariners 1
2000	Yankees 4, Mariners 2
1999	Yankees 4, Red Sox 1
1998	Yankees 4, Indians 2
1997	Indians 4, Orioles 2
1996	Yankees 4, Orioles 1
1995	Indians 4, Mariners 2
1993	Blue Jays 4, White Sox 2

Note: Because of work stoppage, the 1994 ALCS and NLCS were not played.

THE TOP 10

Most Recent NLCS results

YEAR	TEAMS WITH GAMES WON
2003	Marlins 4, Cubs 3
2001	Giants 4, Cardinals 1
2001	Diamondbacks 4, Braves 1
2000	Mets 4, Cardinals 1
1999	Braves 4, Mets 2
1998	Padres 4, Braves 2
1997	Marlins 4, Braves 2
1996	Braves 4, Cardinals 3
1995	Braves 4, Reds 0
1993	Phillies 4, Braves 2

THE TOP 10

Career LCS ERA#

	PITCHER	ERA
1	Mariano Rivera*	.85
2	Orel Hershiser	1.52
3	Randy Johnson*	1.72
4	Fernando Valenzuela	1.95
5	Jim Palmer	1.96
6	Don Sutton	2.02
7	Dave Stewart	2.03
8	Doug Drabek	2.05
9	Ken Holtzman	2.06
10	Tommy John	2.08

Minimum 30 innings pitched

Hershiser pitched in both the NLCS, for the Dodgers and Mets, and the ALCS, for the Indians. He had a 4–0 career LCS record. Palmer was 4–1 in six ALCS appearances with the Baltimore Orioles.

THE TOP 10

Most Career Strikeouts in LCS

	PITCHER	STRIKEOUTS
1	John Smoltz*	71
2	Greg Maddux*	64
3	Tom Glavine*	62
4	Roger Clemens*	61
5	Mike Mussina*	51
6	Orel Hershiser	47
7=	Jim Palmer	46
=	Nolan Ryan	46
9	David Cone*	45
10	David Wells*	42

When your team appears in every NLCS from 1991–99, it also helps. All three of these top strikeout pitchers played for the Atlanta Braves during their remarkable run in the 1990s.

SMOKIN' SMOLTZ

Atlanta's John Smoltz has a 6–2 record with a 2.83 ERA in 17 career NLCS games. He even managed to rack up a save in 1999.

THE DIVISION SERIES

The League Championship Series was established in 1969. Beginning in 1994, Major League Baseball added another layer of playoffs to the postseason. That year, both leagues realigned to form three divisions each (East, Central, West). The champions of each division and a "wild card" team (the second-place team with the best record) move on to play in the best-of-five Divisional Series. The winners of these series then meet in their respective League Championship Series. So far, 20 different teams have made at least one appearance in a Division Series and 16 have won at least once. Not surprisingly, the Yankees (right) and Braves, with six wins each, have won the most Division Series. There have only been nine seasons with Division Series, so we didn't include any top 10s. Stay tuned for further editions!

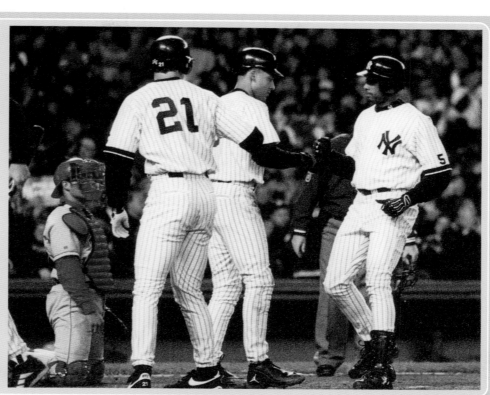

THE TOP 10
Most RBIs in the LCS, Career

PLAYER	RBI
1 David Justice	27
2 Bernie Williams*	22
3= Steve Garvey	21
= John Olerud*	21
5 Reggie Jackson	20
6= George Brett	19
= Graig Nettles	19
8= Fred McGriff*	18
= Paul O'Neill*	18
10= Don Baylor	17
= Ron Gant	17
= Darryl Strawberry	17

Justice is the leader even though he hit only .239 in 46 LCS games. Timing is everything.

THE TOP 10
Best Career Batting Average in the LCS#

PLAYER	PERCENT
1 Will Clark	.468
2 Mickey Rivers	.386
3 Pete Rose	.381
4 Dusty Baker	.371
5 Steve Garvey	.356
6 Brooks Robinson	.348
7 Devon White	.347
8 George Brett	.340
9 Thurman Munson	.339
10 Bernie Williams*	.325

Minimum 50 at-bats

THE TOP 10
Most Home Runs in the LCS, Career

PLAYER	HOME RUNS
1 George Brett	9
2= Steve Garvey	8
= Manny Ramirez	8
4= Darryl Strawberry	7
= Bernie Williams*	7
6= Reggie Jackson	6
= David Justice	6
= Jim Thome*	6
9= Eight players tied with	5

Bernie Williams leaped onto this list with his 3-HR performance in 2001. Williams became the first player to "go yard" in three straight LCS games, including his clutch game-tying blast late in Game 4 of the ALCS.

---

*Active through 2003

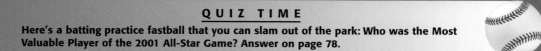

QUIZ TIME
Here's a batting practice fastball that you can slam out of the park: Who was the Most Valuable Player of the 2001 All-Star Game? Answer on page 78.

77

ALL-STAR GAMES

Most Selections to All-Star Teams

PLAYER	SELECTIONS
1 Hank Aaron	25
2 =Willie Mays	24
=Stan Musial	24
4 Mickey Mantle	20
5 =Ted Williams	19
=Cal Ripken, Jr.	19
7 =Yogi Berra	18
=Rod Carew	18
=Al Kaline	18
=Brooks Robinson	18
=Carl Yastrzemski	18

Most Career All-Star Game Hits

PLAYER	HITS
1 Willie Mays	23
2 Stan Musial	20
3 =Nellie Fox	14
=Ted Williams	14
5 =Hank Aaron	13
=Billy Herman	13
=Brooks Robinson	13
=Dave Winfield	13
=Cal Ripken, Jr.	13
10 Al Kaline	12

Most Career All-Star Game Strikeouts

PITCHER	Ks
1 Don Drysdale	19
2 Tom Seaver	16
3 Jim Palmer	14
4 =Jim Bunning	13
=Bob Feller	13
=Catfish Hunter	13
7 =Ewell Blackwell	12
=Juan Marichal	12
=Sam McDowell	12
=Billy Pierce	12

THE SPLENDID SPLINTER
Boston's Ted Williams crosses home plate after slugging a three-run homer in the bottom of the ninth to win the 1941 All-Star Game for the American League.

Recent All-Star Game Results

YEAR	SCORE, LOCATION	MVP
2003	AL 7–NL 6, Chicago	Garret Anderson
2002	AL 7–NL 7, Milwaukee	None
2001	AL 4–NL 1, Seattle	Cal Ripken, Jr.
2000	AL 6–NL 3, Atlanta	Derek Jeter
1999	AL 4–NL 1, Boston	Pedro Martinez
1998	AL 13–NL 8, Colorado	Roberto Alomar
1997	AL 3–NL 1, Cleveland	Sandy Alomar, Jr.
1996	NL 6–AL 0, Philadelphia	Mike Piazza
1995	NL 3–AL 2, Texas	Jeff Conine
1994	NL 8–AL 7, Pittsburgh	Fred McGriff

The All-Star Game is held once each summer at midseason. The starting players for each team, except the pitcher, are chosen by a vote of fans worldwide. The defending league champion managers then select the reserves and the pitching staff. The game has been held every year since 1933. The National League has won 40 All-Star Games to the American League's 32, and there have been two ties.

DID YOU KNOW?
From 1959 through 1962 there were actually two All-Star Games played each year. Heavy rain in the second 1961 game forced the first tie in All-Star Game history.

BALLPARKS, FANS, AND MORE

CANADIAN SHOWPLACE
Of the top 10 largest single-season attendance marks, three were set at the Skydome in Toronto, home of the Blue Jays, which opened in 1989.

BALLPARKS

THE TOP 10

Oldest Current MLB Ballparks

BALLPARK	HOME TEAM	1ST YEAR
1 Fenway Park	Red Sox	1912
2 Wrigley Field	Cubs	1914
3 Yankee Stadium	Yankees	1923
4 Dodger Stadium	Dodgers	1962
5 Shea Stadium	Mets	1964
6 =Edison Field	Angels	1966
=Busch Stadium	Cardinals	1966
8 Network Associates Coliseum	Athletics	1968
9 Kauffman Stadium	Royals	1973
10 Olympic Stadium	Expos	1977

Major League Baseball has had three significant periods of ballpark construction: The 1910s, from which two ballparks survive; the 1960s, which saw several "all-purpose" fields built; and the 1990s, during which nine teams built new ballparks. Many of the newer parks combine the best of today's engineering and architectural techniques and materials with design details that recall the older parks such as Fenway and Wrigley.

THE TOP 10

Former Homes of Teams with Newest Ballparks

BALLPARK	TEAM	YEAR OPENED	FINAL SEASON
1 =Veterans Stadium	Phillies	1971	2003
=Jack Murphy Stadium/ Qualcomm Park	Padres	1969	2003
3 Riverfront Stadium	Reds	1970	2002
4 =Three Rivers Stadium	Pirates	1970	2000
=County Stadium	Brewers	1970	2000
6 =Houston Astrodome	Astros	1965	1999
=3Com/Candlestick Park	Giants	1960	1999
=Tiger Stadium	Tigers	1912	1999
9 Kingdome	Mariners	1977	1999
10 Atlanta-Fulton County Stadium	Braves	1966	1996

Note: The Diamondbacks were an expansion team playing its first season, thus did not have a "former" home. In 1997, the Braves moved into Turner Field. The Phillies, Reds, Pirates, Padres, and Giants moved from multi-purpose stadiums to baseball-only parks. The Houston Astrodome was the first indoor baseball stadium; the first artificial grass was called "AstroTurf."

THE TOP 10

Newest Current MLB Ballparks

BALLPARK	HOME TEAM	1ST YEAR
1 =Citizens Bank Park	Phillies	2004
=Petco Park	Padres	2004
6 Great American Ball Park	Reds	2003
4 =PNC Park	Pirates	2001
=Miller Park	Brewers	2001
6 =Minute Maid Park	Astros	2000
=SBC Park	Giants	2000
=Comerica Park	Tigers	2000
9 Safeco Field	Mariners	1999
10 Bank One Ballpark	Diamondbacks	1998

OPEN SESAME!

Toronto's Skydome (background photo), which opened in 1989, was one of the first parks built with a retractable roof. The stadium boasts a hotel in centerfield whose rooms feature a spectacular view of the field.

THE TOP 10

Largest Spring Training Sites

BALLPARK	LOCATION	TEAM	CAPACITY
1 =Surprise Stadium	Surprise, AZ	Royals and Rangers	10,500
=Scottsdale Stadium	Scottsdale, AZ	Giants	10,500
3 Legends Field	Tampa, FL	Yankees	10,200
4 Hi Corbett Field	Tuscon, AZ	Rockies	10,000
5 HoHoKam Park	Mesa, AZ	Cubs	9,800
6 Diablo Stadium	Tempe, AZ	Angels	9,785
7 Disney's Wide World of Sports Complex	Kissimmee, FL	Braves	9,100
8 Phoenix Municipal Stadium	Phoenix, AZ	Athletics	8,500
9 Fort Lauderdale Stadium	Ft. Lauderdale, FL	Orioles	8,340
10 Space Coast Stadium	Melbourne, FL	Expos	8,100

Baseball prepares for the regular season in February and March, playing in Florida's Grapefruit League and Arizona's Cactus League.

QUIZ TIME

Can you name the Major League expansion team that set a record in 1993 for the highest single-season attendance? Answer on page 82.

THE TOP 10

Smallest Major League Ballparks

	BALLPARK	TEAM	CAPACITY
1	**Fenway Park**	Red Sox	33,871
2	**PNC Park**	Pirates	38,127
3	**Wrigley Field**	Cubs	38,902
4	**Comerica Park**	Tigers	40,120
5	**Kauffman Stadium**	Royals	40,625
6	**SBC Park**	Giants	40,800
7	**Minute Maid Park**	Astros	42,000
8	**Great American Ball Park**	Reds	42,059
9=	**Miller Park**	Brewers	43,000
=	**Citizens Bank Park**	Phillies	43,000

When building a new ballpark, team owners want to strike a balance between a large number of seats and an atmosphere in which all fans can feel like they're a part of the game. PNC Park, for instance, is the second-smallest park, but has a real old-time feel.

Largest MLB Stadiums

	BALLPARK	LOCATION	TEAM	CAPACITY
1	**Yankee Stadium**	New York, NY	Yankees	57,546
2	**Dodger Stadium**	Los Angeles, CA	Dodgers	56,000
3	**Shea Stadium**	New York, NY	Mets	55,601
4	**Skydome**	Toronto, Ont.	Blue Jays	50,516
5	**Coors Field**	Denver, CO	Rockies	50,381
6	**Turner Field**	Atlanta, GA	Braves	49,831
7	**Busch Stadium**	St. Louis, MO	Cardinals	49,676
8	**Ballpark in Arlington**	Arlington, TX	Rangers	49,166
9	**Metrodome**	Minneapolis, MN	Twins	48,678
10	**Oriole Park at Camden Yards**	Baltimore, MD	Orioles	48,262

Pro Player Stadium's capacity can expand to more than 65,000 for big events like the 2003 NLCS (see page 83).

BASEBALL SPRINGS ETERNAL

Spring training is a great way to get a close-up look at Major League players. Smaller stadiums and fine weather are a great combination.

FACTS ABOUT FANS

Highest Single-Season Attendance

	TEAM, YEAR	ATTENDANCE
1	**Rockies**, 1993	4,483,350
2	**Blue Jays**, 1993	4,057,098
3	**Blue Jays**, 1992	4,028,318
4	**Blue Jays**, 1991	4,001,526
5	**Rockies**, 1996	3,891,014
6	**Rockies**, 1992	3,888,453
7	**Braves**, 1993	3,884,720
8	**Rockies**, 1998	3,789.347
9	**Orioles**, 1997	3,711,132
10	**Dodgers**, 1982	3,608,881

SIGN THIS, PLEASE

Tips for autograph seekers: Get there early; be polite; have a pen and what you want signed ready; try to know the players' names; understand that players can't sign forever.

Largest Single-Game Regular-Season Crowds*

	STADIUM, TEAM	DATE	ATTENDANCE
1	**Mile High Stadium**, Colorado Rockies	1993	80,227
2	**Mile High Stadium**, Colorado Rockies	1994	73,957
3	**Cleveland Stadium**, Cleveland Indians	1986	73,303
4	**Cleveland Stadium**, Cleveland Indians	1993	73,290
5	**Mile High Stadium**, Colorado Rockies	1994	73,171
6	**Cleveland Stadium**, Cleveland Indians	1994	72,470
7	**Cleveland Stadium**, Cleveland Indians	1993	72,454
8	**Mile High Stadium**, Colorado Rockies	1993	72,431
9	**Cleveland Stadium**, Cleveland Indians	1993	72,390
10	**Mile High Stadium**, Colorado Rockies	1993	72,208

*Since 1981

Most Seasons Over 3 Million Attendance

	TEAM	SEASONS
1	**Los Angeles Dodgers**	18
2	**Colorado Rockies**	9
3	**St. Louis Cardinals**	7
4	**Atlanta Braves**	6
5=	**New York Yankees**	5
=	**Toronto Blue Jays**	5
7=	**San Francisco Giants**	4
=	**Seattle Mariners**	4
8=	**New York Mets**	2
=	**Arizona Diamondbacks**	2

QUIZ TIME

The New York Yankees have won the most World Series titles. Do you know what university has won the most College World Series titles? See page 84.

THE TOP 10

Largest Single-Game Postseason Crowds

	TEAMS (HOME TEAM SECOND), GAME IN SERIES	DATE	ATTENDANCE
1	**Chicago at Florida**, Game 4	2003	65,829
2	**Houston at Philadelphia**, Game 2	1980	65,476
3	**San Francisco at Florida#**, Game 4	2003	65,464
4	**Chicago at Florida**, Game 5	2003	65,279
5	**Houston at Philadelphia**, Game 1	1980	65,277
6	**Houston at San Diego#**, Game 3	1998	65,235
7	**Chicago at Florida**, Game 3	2003	65,115
8	**Atlanta at San Diego**, Game 4	1998	65,052
9	**Los Angeles at Philadelphia**, Game 4	1977	64,924
10	**Houston at San Diego#**, Game 4	1998	64,898

This list does not include World Series games. For that list, see page 74. These games are all from League Championship Series, except those marked with a #, which are from the Division Series.

THE TOP 10

Coolest Ballpark Food Items

	FOOD	BALLPARK
1	**Bratwurst**	Miller Park
2	**Boog's BBQ**	Oriole Park at Camden Yards
3	**Peanuts in the shell**	Everywhere
4	**Dodger Dog**	Dodger Stadium
5	**Sundae in a helmet**	Everywhere
7	**Rocky Mountain oysters**	Coors Field
7	**Crab Cakes**	Oriole Park at Camden Yards
8	**Gordon Biersch garlic fries**	Pacific Bell Park
9	**Lobster roll**	Tropicana Field
10	**Sushi**	Edison Field (and elsewhere)

This is a completely subjective list; your favorite or coolest item might not be on it. But in our travels throughout the land of baseball, we've come to love these items more than others.

THE TOP 10

Most Popular Ballpark Food Items

FOOD

1	**Hot dogs**
2	**Soda**
3	**Peanuts**
4	**Ice Cream**
5	**Nachos**
6	**Bottled water**
7	**Cotton candy**
8	**Pretzels**
9	**French fries**
10	**Pizza**

"Buy me some peanuts and Cracker Jack..." And a hot dog, a drink, popcorn, and... The Aramark Corporation provides concession services at six Major League stadiums, and these are the food items sold most often at ballparks nationwide.

COMFORT FOOD

A trip to the ballpark just wouldn't be complete without a hot dog smothered in mustard, ketchup, and relish. Fans can get their food at stands throughout ballparks or from vendors roaming the seating areas. Don't forget to watch the game between snacks!

WALK-OFF HOMER

LSU's Warren Morris whoops it up as he rounds the bases after hitting a College World Series–winning home run in 1996.

Recent Cape Cod League Champs

YEAR	TEAM
2003	Orleans Cardinals
2002	Wareham Gatemen
2001	Wareham Gatemen
2000	Brewster Whitecaps
1999	Cotuit Kettleers
1998	Chatham A's
1997	Wareham Gatemen
1996	Chatham A's
1995	Cotuit Kettleers
1994	Wareham Gatemen

Most Recent College World Series Titles

YEAR	SCHOOL
2003	Rice
2002	Texas
2001	Miami (FL)
2000	Louisiana State
1999	Miami (FL)
1998	Southern California
1997	Louisiana State
1996	Louisiana State
1995	Cal State Fullerton
1994	Oklahoma

The annual NCAA College World Series brings the top eight college baseball teams to Omaha, Nebraska, for a round-robin championship.

Recent NBC World Series Winners

YEAR	TEAM
2003	Chinese Taipei
2002	Alaska Goldpanners
2001	Anchorage Glacier Pilots
2000	Liberal (KS) Beejays
1999	Dallas Phillies
1998	El Dorado (KS) Broncos
1997	Mat-Su (AK) Miners
1996	El Dorado (KS) Broncos
1995	Team USA
1994	Kenai (AK) Peninsula Oilers

First played in 1935 and held annually since in August in Wichita, Kansas, the National Baseball Congress World Series is one of the oldest semipro tournaments in the nation.

Most College World Series Titles

SCHOOL	NO. OF TITLES (MOST RECENT)
1 USC	12 (1998)
2=Arizona State	5 (1981)
=Louisiana State	5 (2000)
=Texas	5 (2002)
5 Miami (FL)	4 (2001)
6=Minnesota	3 (1964)
=Arizona	3 (1986)
=Cal State Fullerton	3 (1995)
9=California	2 (1957)
=Michigan	2 (1962)
=Stanford	2 (1988)
=Oklahoma	2 (1994)

AAU Recent Winners

YEAR	TEAM
2002	Dulins Dodgers
2001	Kansas City Monarchs
2000	San Diego Stars
1999	Kansas City Monarchs
1998	West Coast Yankees
1997	Baton Rouge Redsticks
1996	Austin Slam Sox
1995 =	Hartsell NC
=	Knoxville Stars
1994	Continental Blue Streaks
1993	Forest Lake, MN

The Amateur Athletic Union holds national championships in many sports at all age levels. The teams listed here are the champions of the 18-and-under age bracket. Note: Hartsell and Knoxville tied for the title in 1995.

DID YOU KNOW?

Founded in 1885, the Cape Cod League is the oldest of several wood-bat summer leagues that college players use to hone their skills and show off for Major League scouts.

THE TOP 10

Little League World Series First Champions

YEAR	CITY, STATE
1947	Williamsport, PA
1948	Lock Haven, PA
1949	Hammonton, NJ
1950	Houston, TX
1951	Stamford, CT
1952	Norwalk, CT
1953	Birmingham, AL
1954	Schenectady, NY
1955	Morrisville, PA
1956	Roswell, NM

Little League Baseball is the world's largest youth baseball organization, boasting leagues in more than 100 countries. There are different age divisions for boys and girls in both baseball and softball. The Little League division for 11–12 year-olds is the most well known.

THE TOP 10

LLWS States/Countries with Most Titles

	STATE/COUNTRY	TITLES
1	Chinese Taipei	17
2=	Japan	5
=	California	5
4=	New Jersey	4
=	Connecticut	4
=	Pennsylvania	4
7	Mexico	3
8=	Venezuela	2
=	New York	2
=	South Korea	2
=	Texas	2

SOLID SINGLE
Nobuhisa Baba slices a single in the bottom of the sixth inning, scoring two runs and earning Japan the 2001 Little League World Series title, defeating the U.S. champion from Apopka, Florida.

The Ten Most Recent Little League World Series Champions

Country/State/Year

1 Tokyo, Japan, 2003 **2** Louisville, KY, 2002 **3** Tokyo, Japan, 2001 **4** Maracaibo, Venezuela, 2000 **5** Osaka, Japan, 1999 **6** Toms River, NJ, 1998 **7** Guadalupe, Mexico, 1997 **8** Fu-Hsing, Chinese Taipei, 1996 **9** Shan-Hua, Chinese Taipei, 1995 **10** Maracaibo, Venezuela, 1994

Careers of Famous Broadcasters

BROADCASTER	PRIMARY TEAMS	CAREER
1 Vin Scully*	Dodgers	1950–
2 Red Barber	Dodgers, Yankees	1934–66
3 Mel Allen	Yankees	1939–64
4 Harry Caray	Cardinals, White Sox, Cubs	1945–97
5 Ernie Harwell	Tigers	1948–2002
6 Curt Gowdy	Red Sox,	1949–86
7 Jack Buck	Cardinals	1954–2002
8 Ralph Kiner*	Mets	1962–
9 Harry Kalas*	Phillies	1965–
10 Jaime Jarrin*	Dodgers (Spanish)	1959–

Ever since the invention of radio, baseball fans have enjoyed listening to games described by some of the best announcers around. This list is a gathering of the most well-known, listing the careers and primary teams of some of the best "men at the mike." (*Denotes working through 2003 season.)

VOICE OF THE DODGERS
Vin Scully has been telling Dodger fans about their team since the days in Brooklyn.

Hall of Fame Players Turned Broadcasters

	PLAYER	TEAM
1	Richie Ashburn	Phillies
3	Don Drysdale	Angels, Dodgers
4	Al Kaline	Tigers
5	Ralph Kiner	Mets
6	Joe Morgan	ESPN
7	Jim Palmer	Orioles, ABC
8	Phil Rizzuto	Yankees
9	Tom Seaver	Yankees, Mets
10	Duke Snider	Expos

Many former players turn to broadcasting after their careers on the field are over. This list features members of the Hall of Fame who had long careers as full-time broadcasters, as opposed to players who made an occasional appearance on the air. They're listed with the team they broadcast.

Recent Winners of Frick Award

YEAR	BROADCASTER/PRIMARY TEAM	
2003	Bob Uecker,	Brewers
2002	Harry Kalas,	Phillies
2001	Felo Ramirez,	Marlins
2000	Marty Brennaman,	Reds
1999	Arch McDonald,	Senators
1998	Jaime Jarrin,	Dodgers
1997	Jimmy Dudley,	Indians
1996	Herb Carneal,	Twins
1995	Bob Wolff,	Senators
1994	Bob Murphy,	Mets

The Baseball Hall of Fame honors baseball broadcasters with the Ford C. Frick Award, named for the former baseball commissioner. Since 1978, 27 men have been given the award, which was first given to a pair of legendary announcers, Mel Allen and Red Barber. While millions of people have memories of their times at the ballpark, millions more "took part" in baseball's greatest moments through the words and emotions of these men.

PRE-PRESIDENTIAL ADDRESS

Before he enjoyed a career in Hollywood as an actor and a career in politics as a governor and President, Ronald Reagan put his vocal skills to work on radio as a baseball announcer. In those early days of the medium, however, announcers didn't always travel to the games. Instead, Reagan and others "re-created" the game as it was sent to them via telegraph. They would have to make their own sound effects and create their own colorful word pictures of a game that they couldn't see. If the telegraph went down, he would have to make up the game.

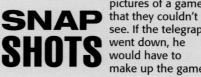

THE TOP 10

Most Recent Winners of Spink Award

YEAR	WRITER/PRIMARY NEWSPAPER
2002	**Hal McCoy**, Dayton Daily News
2001	**Joe Falls**, Detroit Free Press, Detroit News
2000	**Ross Newhan**, Los Angeles Times
1999	**Hal Lebovitz**, Cleveland News and Plain Dealer
1998	**Bob Stevens**, San Francisco Chronicle
1997	**Sam Lacy**, Baltimore Afro-American
1996	**Charles Feeney**, Pittsburgh Post-Gazette
1995	**Joseph Durso**, New York Times
1993	**Wendell Smith**, Pittsburgh Courier
1992	**Leonard Koppett**, N.Y. Post, N.Y. Times, Herald-Tribune

The Hall of Fame recognizes writers for long and dedicated service to baseball, combined with excellence at their craft, with the J.G. Taylor Spink Award, named for the founder of *The Sporting News*. First presented in 1962, the award has since been given to a total of 54 writers, reporters, editors, or columnists.

THE TOP 10

Our Favorite Baseball Movies

	MOVIE	FEATURING	YEAR RELEASED
1	**The Natural**	Robert Redford	1984
2	**Field of Dreams**	Kevin Costner	1989
3	**Bull Durham**	Kevin Costner	1988
4	**Eight Men Out**	John Cusack	1988
5	**Long Gone**	William Petersen	1987
6	**A League of Their Own**	Madonna	1992
7	**The Pride of the Yankees**	Gary Cooper	1942
8	**Bang the Drum Slowly**	Robert DeNiro	1973
9	**Major League**	Charlie Sheen	1989
10	**Bad News Bears**	Walter Matthau	1976

The Natural was based on a novel by Bernard Malamud; in the book, the character played by Redford, Roy Hobbs, doesn't homer at the end of the story, but rather strikes out. *Field of Dreams* also was based on a novel; the "magical" baseball field that Costner's character built is still standing in Dyersville, Iowa, and remains a popular tourist attraction. For *The Pride of the Yankees*, Cooper had to learn to bat, but he was a better actor than a hitter.

THE TOP 10

Our Favorite Baseball Books

	MOVIE	AUTHOR	YEAR PUBLISHED
1	**Total Baseball VII**	Pete Palmer, John Thorn, Michael Gershman	2001
2	**Summer of '49**	David Halberstam	1989
3	**Eight Men Out**	Eliot Asinof	1977
4	**Nine Innings**	Daniel Okrent	1984
5	**The Dickson Baseball Dictionary**	Paul Dickson	2001
6	**The Glory of Their Times**	Lawrence Ritter	1966
7	**Nine Sides of the Diamond**	David Falkner	1990
8	**Good Enough to Dream**	Roger Kahn	1985
9	**Baseball: The Golden Age**	Harold Seymour	1971
10	**Baseball: An Illus. History**	Burns/Ward	1999

A very subjective list. What are your favorites?

THE NATURAL
Robert Redford starred as slugger Roy Hobbs, who had one moment in the sun.

THE TOP 10

Most Recent N.L. Managers of the Year

MANAGER, TEAM

2003	**Jack McKeon**, Marlins
2002	**Tony LaRussa**, Cardinals
2001	**Larry Bowa,** Phillies
2000	**Dusty Baker**, Giants
1999	**Jack McKeon**, Reds
1998	**Larry Dierker**, Astros
1997	**Dusty Baker**, Giants
1996	**Bruce Bochy**, Padres
1995	**Don Baylor**, Rockies
1994	**Felipe Alou**, Expos

This award is based on the performance of a team during the regular season and is normally given to a manager who has "turned around" a team. Voters often look for a manager who, rather than guiding a team of superstars to success, has molded a younger team to new heights or inspired a team with a poor record one year to become a winner the next.

GIANT OF A MANAGER

Former Dodgers outfielder Dusty Baker became the manager of the Giants in 1993 and has led them to the playoffs twice.

THE COMMISSIONER

This book does not contain a list of the top 10 Major League Baseball commissioners for one good reason: There have only been nine. The office of Commissioner was created in 1920 following the Black Sox scandal in the 1919 World Series. Judge Kenesaw Mountain Landis (left) was named the first to hold the office, which oversees all aspects of Major League Baseball. He held the job until 1944. Other former commissioners include Ford Frick, Bowie Kuhn, former Los Angeles Olympics chief Peter Ueberroth, former Yale president A. Bartlett Giamatti, and Fay Vincent. Currently, the Commissioner is Allan H. "Bud" Selig, the former president of the Milwaukee Brewers.

SNAP SHOTS

THE TOP 10

Most Recent A.L. Managers of the Year

MANAGER, TEAM

2003	**Tony Peña**, Royals
2002	**Mike Scioscia**, Angels
2001	**Lou Piniella**, Mariners
2000	**Jerry Manuel**, White Sox
1999	**Jimy Williams**, Red Sox
1998	**Joe Torre**, Yankees
1997	**Davey Johnson**, Orioles
1996	= **Johnny Oates**, Rangers
	= **Joe Torre**, Yankees
1995	**Lou Piniella**, Mariners
1994	**Buck Showalter**, Yankees

Like the National League award, this award is named via a vote of the members of the Baseball Writers Association of America. There is one winner for each league.

DID YOU KNOW?

Hall of Fame catcher Yogi Berra became a manager with the Yankees and Mets. One of his most famous sayings was "It ain't over 'til it's over." Now, Yogi, this book is over.

THE TOP 10

Satchel Paige's Rules on How to Stay Young

1 Avoid fried meats which angry up the blood.

2 If your stomach disputes you, lie down and pacify it with cool thoughts.

3 Keep the juices flowing by jangling around gently as you move.

4 Go very light on the vices, such as carrying on in society. The social ramble ain't restful.

5 Avoid running at all times.

6 Don't look back. Something might be gaining on you.

Ol' Satch, the great Negro League and Major League pitcher, only came up with six in this famous "list for living," which is etched into the stone over his grave. But we won't hold that against him.

THE TOP 10

Most Recent Number-One Draft Picks

PLAYER, POSITION, TEAM

2003	**Delmon Young**, OF, Devil Rays
2002	**Bryan Bullington**, P, Pirates
2001	**Joe Mauer**, C, Twins
2000	**Adrian Gonzalez**, 1B, Marlins
1999	**Josh Hamilton**, OF, Devil Rays
1998	**Pat Burrell**, 3B, Phillies
1997	**Matt Anderson**, P, Tigers
1996	**Kris Benson**, P, Pirates
1995	**Darin Erstad**, OF, Angels
1994	**Paul Wilson**, P, Mets

Each June, Major League Baseball holds its annual amateur draft. Players are drafted as seniors in high school, or after they have completed three seasons in college. It is very rare for even a very high draft pick to jump directly to the big leagues. The first amateur draft was held in 1965.

THE TOP 10

First Ten Number-One Draft Picks

PLAYER, POSITION, TEAM

1965	**Rick Monday**, OF, Athletics
1966	**Steve Chilcott**, P, Mets
1967	**Ron Blomberg**, 1B, Yankees
1968	**Tim Foli**, SS, Mets
1969	**Jeff Burroughs**, OF, Senators
1970	**Mike Ivie**, C, Padres
1971	**Danny Goodwin**, C, White Sox
1972	**Dave Roberts**, 3B, Padres
1973	**David Clyde**, P, Rangers
1974	**Bill Almon**, SS, Padres

THE TOP 10

Herb Pennock's Ten Commandments of Pitching

1 Develop your faculty of observation.

2 Conserve your energy.

3 Make contact with players, especially catchers and infielders, and listen to what they have to say.

4 Work everlastingly for control.

5 When you are on the field, always have a baseball in your hand and don't slouch around. Run for a ball.

6 Keep studying the hitters for their weak and strong points. Keep talking with your catchers.

7 Watch your physical condition and your mode of living.

8 Always pitch to the catcher and not the hitter. Keep your eye on that catcher and make him your target before letting the ball go.

9 Find your easiest way to pitch, your most comfortable delivery and stick to it.

10 Work for what is called a rag arm. A loose arm can pitch overhanded, side arm, three quarter, underhanded, any old way, to suit the situation at hand.

HINTS FROM HERB

Pennock was a Hall-of-Fame pitcher with the Athletics, Red Sox, and Yankees from 1912–36. He wrote this list sometime in the 1940s.

INDEX

INDEX

INDEX

PHOTO CREDITS

1	Wood: Vesely/MLB Photos
8–9	Mickey Mantle: AP/Wide World; Martinez: Michael Zagaris/MLB Photos
10–11	Aaron, Ruth/Gehrig: AP/Wide World
12–13	McGwire: Rich Pilling/MLB Photos; Maris: AP/Wide World
14–15	Ripken: Brad Mangin/MLB Photos;Gehrig: AP/Wide World
16–17	Clemens:David Durochik/MLB Photos; Louis Deluca/MLB Photos; Young: National Baseball Library
18–19	Smith: Don Smith/MLB Photos
20–21	Robinson: Corbis/Bettmann; Vizquel: Rich Pilling/MLB Photos
22–23	Jones: Allen Kee/MLB Photos; Rodriguez: John Williamson/MLB Photos
24–25	Mays (2): AP/Wide World
26–27	Buckner: Rich Pilling/MLB Photos; Clemente: MLB/Photofile
28–29	Wambsganns: National Baseball Library; Roberts: AP/Wide World
30–31	Piazza: Stephen Green/MLB Photos;
	Hornsby: National Baseball Library
32–33	1939 class: National Baseball Library; Koufax: AP/Wide World
34–35	Gibson, Ward: National Baseball Library; Paige: AP/Wide World
36–37	Harris: MLB Photos
38–39	Zwilling: National Baseball Library; Van Landingham: Brad Mangin/MLB
40–41	Gehrig: AP/Wide World; Cloninger: Corbis/Bettmann
42–43	Paige: AP/Wide World; Jays: MLB Photos
44–45	Renteria: Rich Pilling/MLB Photos
46–47	Yankees: AP/Wide World; Torre: Stephen Green/MLB Photos
48–49	Schmidt: Rich Pilling/MLB Photos; Lofton: AP/Wide World
50–51	Walker, Wills: AP/Wide World
52–53	Game: AP/Wide World; Crawford: National Baseball Library
54–55	Mascots (2): MLB Photos; Pennant: Russ McConnell
56–57	O'Malley: AP/Wide World; Park: Brad Mangin/MLB Photos
58	Suzuki: John Williamson/MLB Photos;
	Cuban players: AP/Wide World
60–61	Bonds, Mussina: AP/Wide World
62–63	Williams: MLBP; Ruth: AP/Wide World
64	Cone: David Seelig/MLB Photos
66–67	Yankees: AP/Wide World; Hernandez: Michael Zagaris/MLB Photos; Trophy: MLB Photos
68–69	Stengel/Mantle, Berra: AP/Wide World
70–71	Jackson, Tenace: AP/Wide World
72–73	Whitey Ford: MLB Photos; Mathewson: National Baseball Library
74–75	Mazeroski, McCarthy: AP/Wide World
76–77	Smoltz: Stephen Green/MLB; Williams: Rich Pilling/MLB
78	Williams: AP/Wide World
80–81	Skydome: Robert Skeoch/MLB Photos; Spring training: MLB Photos
82–83	Fans, kid: Rich Pilling/MLB
84–85	College World Series, Little League World Series: AP/Wide World
86–87	Scully: Bob Rosato/MLB; Reagan: AP/Wide World
88–89	Pennock: AP/Wide World; Landis: National Baseball Library; Baker: MLB Photos

SOURCES

As noted in the Introduction, most of the statistical information in this book came from Major League Baseball's official Web site, www.mlb.com. Other information was gleaned from *Total Baseball*, the official encyclopedia of Major League Baseball.

The Elias Sports Bureau in New York City is the official statistician for Major League Baseball. They provided MLB with all the stats listed on the Web site as well as all records kept and distributed by MLB during the regular season and postseason. Elias also provided us directly with some Top 10s, including those relating to game length.

The Society for American Baseball Research (SABR) was very helpful, providing assistance in locating some of the more obscure information. Special thanks to Jim Charlton for his help.

The Web sites www.baseball-almanac.com and www.latinobaseball.com and the Baseball Hall of Fame archive library on-line were also sources for some material. Web sites for the National Baseball Congress, Little League Baseball, and the Amateur Athletic Union also provided information.

The Sporting News Complete Baseball Record Book, another official Major League Baseball publication, was a font of information. We used the 2001 edition.

Other books we consulted while searching for our information included *Baseball Timeline*, by Burt Solomon, a day-by-day history of baseball; *The Series*, a complete record of the World Series, including box scores of every game, published by *The Sporting News*; *Blackball Stars* by John B. Holway, a history of Negro League Baseball; *A Whole New Ball Game: The Story of the All-American Girls Professional Baseball League*, by Sue Macy.

ACKNOWLEDGMENTS

Special thanks to Eric Enders at the National Baseball Hall of Fame for his outstanding ninth-inning fact-checking.

At DK, thanks to editors Beth Hester and Beth Sutinis.

Thanks to Rich Pilling and Paul Cunningham of Major League Baseball Photos, Carolyn McMahon at AP/Wide World Photos, and Bill Burdick at the National Baseball Hall of Fame.

Special thanks to the the broad-backed Chris Koeper of the Santa Barbara Foresters for posing for our cover photo.

For providing all of us fans with another amazing season, full of record-breaking feats and memorable, historic games, thanks to all the players, coaches, and teams of Major League Baseball.

AUTHORS' BIOGRAPHIES

James Buckley, Jr., has written more than 35 books about sports for young people and adults, including *Eyewitness Baseball, The Visual Dictionary of Baseball, Baseball: A Celebration*, and *Perfect: The Story of Baseball's 16 Perfect Games*. He is the editorial director of the Shoreline Publishing Group, based in Santa Barbara, California.

David Fischer, a New Jersey-based author, has written several sports books, including *A Thing or Two About Baseball, Do Curve Balls Really Curve?*, and *The 50 Coolest Jobs in Sports*. He has been published in *Sports Illustrated for Kids, The New York Times,* and *Yankees Magazine*, and has worked for *Sports Illustrated*, NBC Sports, and The National Sports Daily.